NOT ALL CAME BACK

A Somerset farmer's son at Gallipoli

Anton Bantock

NOT ALL CAME BACK

A Somerset farmer's son at Gallipoli

Anton Bantock

First published in 2010 by

The MALAGO Society
www.malago.org.uk
and Redcliffe Press Ltd,
81g Pembroke Road, Bristol, BS8 3EA
www.redcliffepress.co.uk
info@redcliffepress.co.uk

© Anton Bantock

ISBN 978-1-906593-62-9

Design and typesetting by André Coutanche
Printed and bound by Hobbs The Printers Ltd, Totton, Hampshire

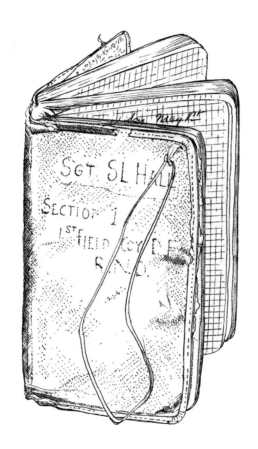

FOREWORD

SOMETIME IN THE EARLY 1980s a small battered attaché case came into my hands. It contained the diary, pocket book and letters of Sydney Hall, written from Gallipoli in 1915. It also contained all the letters written to him by his father, mother, sisters and brother and numerous friends and relations during that campaign.

All these items had been gathered together after Sydney's death in July 1915 and treasured by his family. By the 1980s only one of his close relatives, his sister Dorothy Hall, remained alive. She allowed me to photocopy all these manuscripts and, with the help of a magnifying glass, we managed to decipher all the crucial entries written in pencil in his pocket book. Before she died in 1987 at the age of 96, Dorothy Hall told me that her brother's grave was to be found in the Lancashire Landings cemetery at Cape Helles. In August 1988 I went to Gallipoli and found the small rectangular tablet among thousands of others in some six cemeteries at the extreme end of the Gallipoli peninsula maintained by the Commonwealth War Graves Commission.

In 1990 I returned again, taking with me all the photocopies, and with the help of a Turkish friend, Ali Findikoglou, who kindly drove me miles over the terrain on the carrier of his motorbike, we made detailed maps of the trench systems, ramps and landing stages constructed by the men of the Royal Naval Division. In the evenings, in Ali's modest 'pansiyon' in Seddülbahir, I wrote up the story of Sydney Hall. Here we have in microcosm a complete reconstruction of five tortured months in 1915, in which the horrors of the front line come into brutal confrontation with the orderly, timeless life of a gentleman farmer and his family in North Somerset.

What the letters tell us about village life during those five months during the second year of the Great War is no less remarkable than the spirit of the men out there in Gallipoli confronting with heroism and even humour a dawning tragic and hopeless military disaster.

Fillwood Farm, its great sixteenth-century farmhouse, outbuildings, pastures, orchards, tennis court and woodland, has now vanished without trace under a great tidal wave of bricks and mortar as Bristol's southern suburbs advanced into rural Somerset.

The Gallipoli peninsula is now a national park. Apart from the military cemeteries, on beaches, clifftops and often shaded by clumps of pine trees whose needles sing in the stiff breezes off the Aegean Sea, there is nobody there - a sublime peace and emptiness has returned to the place of so much human turmoil and suffering.

This profile of one young man who died there is dedicated to all those countless others whose names are recorded in those cemeteries, but whose stories now can never be told.

AB
January 2010

ACKNOWLEDGEMENTS

W E ARE INDEBTED to the Hall family for permission to publish these manuscripts and for the loan of photographs and other memorabilia. Thanks are due to Christine Lillington who typed the first draft in 1991 and has re-typed it in its present format in 2009. Parts of the narrative in a condensed form were first published in instalments in the 'MALAGO' magazine in a series entitled 'Bishopsworth Heroes', which included the record of several other servicemen whose names are recorded on the First World War memorial in St Peter's Church, Bishopsworth, Bristol.

This is a joint publication between the Malago Society (the local history society for south-west Bristol) and Redcliffe Press, and we are grateful to those who have made this project happen, especially André and Marie Jo Coutanche of the Malago Society and John and Angela Sansom of Redcliffe Press.

Finally, Anton Bantock, who has been responsible for so much original local history research (notably the definitive history of the Smyth family of Ashton Court) researched, wrote and encouraged the publication of this book and drew the line drawings.

The picture on the front cover is by Charles E. Brock R.I. (1870-1938) and is entitled 'Home Again'. This illustration was published in 1918 by Abdulla & Co.

INTRODUCTION

THE FIRST INDICATION of the Great War in Bishopsworth, Somerset, in the days before radio, telephone and the bus service, was the arrival of a horse-drawn mail van outside the old Post Office. On the sides of the van had been pasted huge posters announcing 'WAR WITH GERMANY'. To most village people in North Somerset the events taking place in Bosnia, and even in Belgium, must have seemed incredibly remote. On Sunday 28th June 1914, the day that Archduke Franz Ferdinand was assassinated at Sarajevo, the Patronal Festival had been celebrated in St Peter's church, with all the accustomed extras - a tea for children on the vicarage lawn and games afterwards in Mr Gardiner's field at Bishport Lodge.

Mr Ford, the vicar, had an inkling perhaps of what was going on. He appealed in the parish magazine for all communicants to join in his special prayers of intercession after communion, 'at this time of threatened danger', but the dangers of Civil War in Ireland and the 'spoilation' of the Church through recent Government acts of disestablishment were probably more on his mind than the possibility of a major European conflagration.

Revd and Mrs Ford

At the end of the last week in July, Edwin Wyatt - a dapper little bachelor who lived at Home Farm with his brother Arthur and sister-in-law, Lizzie - wrote a footnote in his church almanac: 'War between Austria and Serbia began this week; feared lest other nations should become involved, perhaps England, tho' hope not'.

The 3rd August was a Bank Holiday. Edwin wrote: 'By brake to Wrington. Cricket match, lunch and tea; back wet, late by train. Stormy day; v. heavy rain in evening. England and Germany declaration of war'. For the time being life went on as if nothing had happened.

'Office till 5.20. Home for tea; cricket field and garden'. Edwin was chief cashier at the firm of Bristol solicitors, Burges, Ware & Salmon in Marsh Street, and at 65 he had lost none of his drive. Meetings of the Fourth Building Society, the Church Missionary Society, the local Conservative Association, the Harvest Festival Committee and the village Fire Brigade occupied most evenings; not to mention the Parish Council, choir practice on Friday evenings, the cricket pitch on Saturday afternoons and croquet matches on the vicarage lawn.

Old friends died - Mr Rossiter of The Grange and Mr Hensler - and younger ones got married. Grace Moon of the 'School' became engaged to Sidney Gardiner of The Lodge, and Edwin's pretty, musical niece, Winifred Hall, married Will Evans and set up home in Knowle.

Edwin Light Wyatt

Edwin was a member of 'The Good Old Friends', a society which undertook Alpine hiking holidays each year, but that August they had to cancel their tour because of the European situation. In fact, they never met again.

By September, the full force of the emergency had begun to dawn on the village. Mr Ford began his monthly letter to his parishioners: 'My dear friends, the terrible war in which we are engaged has compelled us to alter several of our parochial arrangements ...'. The Harvest Festival, which had been fixed for 9th September (because that was the only day Mr Cole could attend with his steam roundabouts) was cancelled. The enormous recruiting campaign mounted in Bristol soon began to have its effect on Bishopsworth.

The North Somerset branch of the Parliamentary Recruiting Committee held its meetings in the schoolroom and Edwin Wyatt served as chairman. The predictable, high-sounding sentiments were expressed by the official speakers: 'Our part in this war is not only to vindicate the right of Belgium to her rights and existence, but also to vindicate the similar rights of other small nations ...'. The other speaker said, 'Suitable men are perhaps holding back because they think that up to the present we are doing well. For us to lose the war means the losing of all we hold most dear'.

At the outbreak of war, Edwin's boss, Colonel W.E. Burges, having served in the Boer War and later commanded the 3rd Battalion of the Gloucestershire Regiment, was placed in charge of the Bristol Recruiting Centre at the Colston Hall. Within three weeks he had raised over 5,000 troops. On 15th September the people of Bristol were overjoyed to hear that Colonel Burges had been appointed to command the new Bristol Battalion of the Gloucesters, called thereafter 'Bristol's Own'.

Response to the recruiting campaign in Bishopsworth was brisk. From farm and mine, workshop and factory, the young men of North Somerset flocked to enlist, some from a desire to do their bit for the country and others for more mundane economic reasons. There had been serious unemployment in country districts, added to which the war, with the prospects of France and the Near East, seemed gloriously different and exciting, an escape from the deadly round of village hops in the school hall, the pub or the miners' club.

A typical response came from Maurice Moon, son of the village schoolmaster, and apprenticed to Goldsmiths Assurance Jewellers at the bottom of Park Street, Bristol. When war broke out he was staying at Fillwood Farm, as his parents were away on holiday. Dorothy Hall later recalled, 'I was upstairs changing my dress when a voice shouted, "Dor, are you there?". I came down and found it was Maurice and Reg Quick. "Whatever are you up to?" I asked. It was midday and normally they would have been at work, but there they were in moth-eaten khaki. "And what do you intend to do in that?" I said. "To have six months' holiday at the Government's expense," he said. Reg Quick worked for the Waterworks. He was very good-looking and I was quite gone on him'.

To these young men, Edwin Wyatt was much more than secretary of the North Somerset Recruiting Committee. He was the father figure to whom they dutifully went to take their leave and to whom they wrote letters from the front.

Jack Lukins from the upper village joined the Somerset Light Infantry, as did Albert Hall from King's Head cottages. Ernest Sweet of Upton Farm, Dundry, joined the North Somerset Yeomanry; Maurice Moon of the school house the Ambulance Corps; Joe Simmons of Gaston Cottage the 6th Gloucesters and Joe Hill, the Royal Garrison Artillery. For Edwin, the greatest wrench was parting with his two protégés, Cecil and Gerald Hill, both choirboys and the sons of P.C. Hill who rented Swiss Cottage in Chapel Lane from him.

A list of all those who enlisted was written on a board and placed beneath the Union Flag at the west end of the church. As the list grew longer, another factor entered the recruitment drive, namely the fear of 'being left out'.

Meanwhile, as part of the village's war effort, Mrs Ford, the vicar's wife, organised work parties of women who met at the vicarage on Monday afternoons to make clothes for the Red Cross.

Weeks and months passed and, as the casualties mounted, the newspapers were avidly searching for news. The first man from Bishopsworth to fall in battle was Jack Lukins, in June 1915. Seriously wounded on the Western Front, he was taken to Boulogne hospital and it was reported 'he died of exhaustion following haemorrhage'. A medical officer who attended him recalled that Jack said before losing consciousness, 'Well, sir, I only be one of Kitchener's Army, but I'd sooner come out here and have these wounds and know I've done my bit, than stay at home'.

The same month a cutting appeared in Edwin Wyatt's scrapbook. 'KILLED IN ACTION. May 13th 1915. Sweet, Ernest John, of R Squadron, North Somerset Yeomanry. Second and dearly loved son of Mr & Mrs John Sweet of Upton Farm, Dundry, aged 24'. 'He was a daredevil', Philip Golding said in 1990 when he was 102. He was recalling the days when they were all young men together on the Dundry farms. 'We were a rough lot. We used to work off surplus energy with the boxing gloves in the hay barn'.

The recruiting officer from the North Somerset Yeomanry made a visit. 'We want one of you lot', he said. Philip wanted to go, but he had lost a finger in the chaff cutter and couldn't fire a rifle, so Ernest Sweet volunteered. 'He was far too venturesome, couldn't keep down', said Philip. 'Took a look over the top and got a bullet through the head'.

The arrival of wounded and maimed soldiers in the locality was slowly bringing home the horrors of the Western Front. One girl recalled the convalescent soldiers, dressed in hospital blue, sitting in the sun in Leigh Woods. 'One of them came up to my mother and asked permission to touch me. "I have a little girl like her at home", he said. Mother said he could, forgetting for the moment the fact that he was "the enemy".'

So it was that war came to Bishopsworth ...

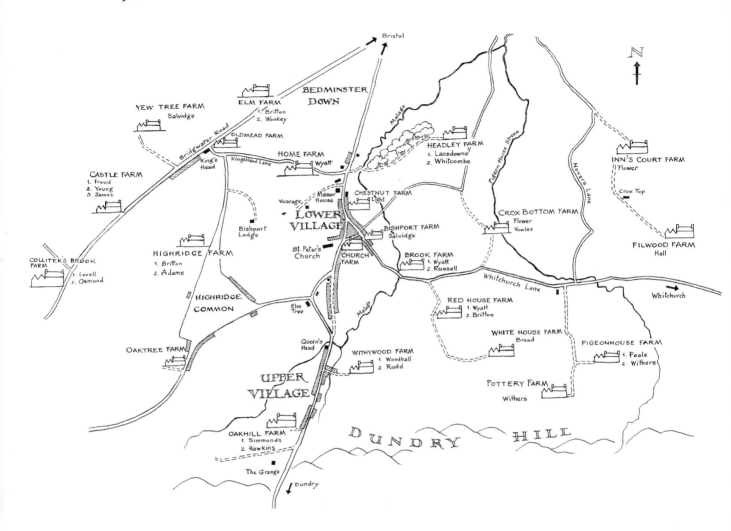

BISHOPSWORTH FARMS c.1920

The Somerset village of Bishopsworth as it was in the early twentieth century. The centre of Bristol is three miles to the north-east. The farms in and around the village formed a social network of inter-related families who constituted the local gentry. Fillwood Farm, the home of the Hall family, is on the east of the map

EDWIN WYATT wrote in his almanac, 'Syd Hall here to tea'. Sydney Llewellyn Hall, his nephew, was 21. He was the elder son of Benjamin and Clara Hall of Fillwood Farm *(above)*. He was born in 1893 and his Christian names were a break with tradition, for elder sons of the Hall family had been 'Benjamin' for generations. 'We've had enough of Benjamins,' said his father. 'Sydney' must have been chosen by his mother after her favourite brother, Sydney Wyatt, and 'Llewellyn' after Colonel Llewellyn, the Conservative and Unionist Member of Parliament for North Somerset, which establishes the political loyalties of the family.

The Halls had farmed Fillwood's 800 acres since the sixteenth century. The property, situated on rising ground to the south of Bristol and overlooked from the west by the long, bold outline of Dundry Hill, had a distinguished lineage. The Romans had a settlement on the site and there is a tradition that in medieval times it was a hunting lodge in the Royal Forest of Fillwood. It was probably the lost manor of Filton (or Philton) and came into the hands of the Smyths of Ashton Court in the 1570s. From them it passed to the Temples of Newton Park and remained part of their estate until most of their farms were sold in 1924.

The farmhouse was a building of tremendous antiquity - so old that it had become part of the landscape. Its bulging gabled walls, pierced by small mullioned windows, were shored up by massive buttresses. Each gable was crowned, in the tradition of North Somerset, with a large stone ball or 'Death's Head'. From the parlour a cavernous chimney rose through the core of the house and was cleaned once a year by hauling a gorse bush through it tied onto a length of rope. On the walls hung two muskets and a rapier which had been there since time past memory.

Ben and Clara Hall were typical of the North Somerset farming community. It was still the age in which farmers were lesser gentry. They were leaders of the community, pillars of the church and united by interest, and certainly in North Somerset, by blood. Rural society was still rigidly divided into 'masters' and 'men', and the farmers were the 'masters'. They were, for the most part, well educated. They sent their sons to grammar schools and their daughters to private establishments in Clifton or Knowle. They employed two or more servants in the house, as well as the regular farmhands. Every Sunday their traps and carriages could be seen tied up outside the church. They sat on the parish council, were overseers of the poor, members of the local school board, read the lessons in church, dispensed charity and were generally looked up to by lesser folk. In the evenings they congregated in each other's homes and, while their elders held whist drives, the younger members organised tennis tournaments, for no self-respecting farm was without its well-tended lawn.

Ben Hall was a tall, taciturn man possessed of a lively mischievous streak, especially in his youth, but after 1914 he did not enjoy good health. In a more educated age he would have been an engineer, for he was a lesser genius when it came to tackling defective farm machinery. Sydney inherited this ability from his father, as well as his sparkle, though in his case it was usually more on the surface than beneath.

Clara Hall was the youngest of the large family of Wyatts of Home Farm. For the daughter of a small farmer she had an enlightened education. One of her elder brothers, Joseph, a missionary in Southern India, had paid for her to attend a private school in Clifton, and a letter to her recommending uplifting literature establishes her credentials as a member of the educated elite. He wrote:

You said you don't think you should like Dickens because you don't like 'Bleak House'. Don't trouble yourself about 'Bleak House', it is one of his poorest so I give you credit for not liking it. But as soon as possible get 'Pickwick' for till you have read that you have a treat before you. Dickens wrote it when he was about 23 years old and it is considered his best. When you have read it, tell me how many times you laughed over it and how heartily you laughed.

The Waverleys that you have read are good, but there is a great deal of Scotch in them and on that account many people lose interest in them. 'Guy Mannering' is good, and so is 'Old Mortality' and 'The Heart of Midlothian', but before you read these, you ought to read 'Ivanhoe' which is one of Scott's English novels.

Do you read any poetry? There is a very large stock of good poetry which you ought to read. For example, Tennyson's 'Maud' and 'In Memoriam' and also 'The Princess' by the same author. There is a new book of his just out called 'The Holy Grail' which caused a great stir. You might, I think, borrow all these books from Mrs Randall or some other friends. Then you ought, if possible, to read some of Coleridge's poetry; one remarkable piece of his is called 'The Ancient Mariner'. You know, of course, Keble's 'Christian Year', Milton's 'Paradise Lost', Cowper and parts of Longfellow ... If you have not read the first of these - 'The Christian Year' - you must please at once buy a copy for about 2/6d and place it on my account.

Ben Hall and family at Fillwood Farm. Sydney is on the left, next to Dorothy ('Dor').
Winifred ('Win') has her arm on her father's shoulder. Antony is rubbing his eye, and
Phyllis, on her mother's lap, died aged 8

Sydney had two sisters - Winifred (born 1888) and Dorothy (born 1890) - and a younger brother, Antony (born 1898). A younger sister, Phyllis (born 1900) died of appendicitis when she was eight. There exists a delightful photograph of the family taken about 1904 *(above)*. Antony, made to look too long into the sun, is rubbing his eyes. Win and Dor (which is how they were known) are wearing glossy velveteen dresses and have their long hair in ribbons. Sydney, aged 10, in Norfolk jacket and breeches, lace-up boots and stiff collar, was very much the life and soul of the family. Self-possessed, superbly confident with inner fires burning and sometimes erupting into bursts of hilarity, as bright as a new button.

Sydney went to Merrywood Grammar School and in 1910 won a City University scholarship to enter the Merchant Venturers Technical College at Bristol University to read mechanical engineering. He was beloved of his many relations and cycled all over the county to visit them, especially young lady cousins who competed for his favours. A special favourite was Margie Wyatt, the eldest daughter of Clara's brother John, who farmed at Claverham, near Yatton. After a visit there in January 1910 he wrote (on black-edged paper, following the death of Edward VII):

Dear Auntie,

I have got home! I bethought me that while I was in the district I ought to call on Arthur as I did not see him on Tuesday. So I did a right wheel and landed in Cleeve. I saw Arthur after going into the fields to search, and then came home, calling at the Castle as I did so. I thus completed the journey in 2½ hours.

Found them threshing, so changed and went out (and pretended to work). Then knocked off, put myself pretty and marched off to Knowle. Arrived there, I distinguished myself by winning the 'booby' prize which was a nice little buttonhole flower holder. Received an ovation for playing so well. Then followed 'music' and very nice it was too; they called it 'Refusal' and 'Postman's Knock'. Quite a new kind; kicked off in high spirits at 12.30 and got home at one (shocking). Went to bed and to sleep and woke up again and, finding the rain had released me from the necessity of working, I am sat down and write this 'twoddle'. Here endeth the adventures of S.H. (Sherlock Holmes).

This is to give notice. My best thanks are due to you and Uncle for having me to stay with you, to the two girls for amusing me and to Joseph for lending me half his bed. I will be pleased to share mine with him. I told Antony that Margie wanted him and he declared himself entranced, and says he is dying to see her next week, spending a day in her company, if he is allowed to (I do envy him). He is rich now, has just sent up 100 moleskins and received 15/8.

Dorothy got an invitation to stay at Knowle, so she did. Just about enjoying herself, I should think. Lovely weather! Makes me feel quite poetical. Reminds me of the beautiful rhyme: Pitter, patter ... After so much horribly dry weather too. Am quite at a loss for anything to say or do, so I had better dry up. With love and kisses for all who want them, out of the superabundance received last night, I beg to remain,

Your beloved and loving nephew,

Sydney

For Margie was enclosed a studio photo of himself in academic dress, wearing a solemn expression. At 17 he was tall and slender with a refined, almost delicate expression which disguised an inner resolve and determination. There was talk of a European war as early as 1911 and Sydney, in a surge of patriotism, joined the University's division of the Officer Training Corps. In

1912 he won a B.Sc. degree with first class honours and was awarded an industrial bursary by the Royal Commissioners for the 1851 Exhibition, to the value of £100.

On the back of another photo of himself, this time at his graduation ceremony, he wrote:

Fillwood Farm, Christmas Eve, 1912
Dear Margie,

So sorry I didn't see you when you were up, but it was so unexpected that I couldn't arrange. Give my fondest and best to Uncle and Auntie Gladys, and Joseph, and keep the rest. Merry Christmas and Happy New Year. Sydney.

The Hall family with Sydney (seated, right) in his teens. Parents Ben and Clara are seated left and centre. Standing (L to R): Win, Antony and Dor

Sydney worked for a year at the Bristol Waggon & Carriage Works and then with the firm of Stothert & Pitt in Bath. When war came in August 1914 it was a foregone conclusion that he would enlist. He would do his bit for King and Country. He was a natural leader and his special skills were much in demand. His views on the war were probably much the same as Jai Ran, an Indian engineering student whom he had come to know at Bristol University, and who wrote to him in February 1915:

Camp Shiggar
Dear Hall,

Your letter written from NCO's mess was not a surprise to me because I had thought all of you - I mean fellows like you - must have gone in to fight, and especially when I had not received a letter from you for a long time. I had become almost sure that you must be in Egypt or in France, fighting <u>wisely</u> and <u>bravely</u> for I had received a letter some time ago from Orr, who if you know him, was a 2nd year student when I left college. He was for some time working as a demonstrator - also in the Physical lab. He informed me that he gave up engineering matters and took to military studies and was successful insomuch as to get a commission. He had also informed me that most of the passed-out fellows had joined the army.

I expect you would like to know what the people here think of the war. More conservative and religious sections think that Christianity has practically taught people nothing but to cut each others throat for a piece of land or metal; more informed think that England did the right thing to join the war for her own honour and safety, more than for Belgium.

Nobody is doubtful as to the ultimate result, but as you say, the achievement is beastly difficult. If it is certain that we must be victorious, it is also well nigh impossible to crush Germany completely and without complete crushing of Germany perhaps there will be no peace - not a permanent one at least. From one point of view this war is a blessing in disguise, there will be a united British Empire; there will be more sympathy between white, black and brown; the White Serpent will not be worshipped when he is hidden in the sleeve ready to give the severest bite. I believe it has been proved beyond doubt that several Germans holding responsible positions in India (to the exclusion of Indians) and other British possessions, were really spies, and in spite of all that, their spying has been a complete failure.

They perhaps had counted upon Indian unrest, Home Rule trouble etc. and had also perhaps thought that they would be exciting Indian and Egyptian mussalmans when they contributed to bring in the poor Turks.

I suppose if you had gone to France by this time, this letter will be opened by one of your family members. I take this opportunity to send them my best compliments and wish them your happy return home victorious, and jolly as ever.

Whenever you find an opportunity, please send me a word of your health and safety. If possible write something about the Indian soldier. I wish I could get there to see for myself.

I am, your old and sincere friend, Jai Ran. (Assistant Engineer, Dharwar P.W.D. Bombay Presidency, India).

Please excuse this bad ink - I can't get any better here and have run out of my stock.

The last request is interesting. Sydney was to see much of the sterling qualities of the Indian soldier in action, but whether or not he ever wrote to Jai Ran about them, we shall never know.

However, he did not go to France or Egypt as Jai Ran imagined. He joined the Divisional Engineers of the Royal Naval Division (RND - RNDDE), which functioned like any other division of the British Army, though its ranks, commands and traditions were those of the Royal Navy. He was posted to Deal in Kent and underwent intensive NCO training.

Okney Bottom, 4 Oct. 1914

Dear Margie,

Thanks so much for your kind and thoughtful letter. Please don't apologise for writing to me, I can stand these things occasionally.

I explain my reiterated instructions as being due to a pronounced military habit. I have to instruct men 8 hours a day and repeat for 8 hours next day, and so on. I hope you don't need quite 8 hours a day and expect that after the present reminder, that further instructions will be entirely unnecessary and that I shall find substantial improvement when I see you. Any more to say? Am doing quite well and having a good time. Have just done the hardest Sunday's work I remember. Just done at 7 o'c.

Hope you are all well, Cheerio, Syd

He was probably overdoing it when he damaged his arm, but at Christmas he was writing:

Fillwood. 24.xii.14

Dear Margie,

Also Auntie, Uncle, Gladdie and Josie, in fact to all.

You see I'm home again. Have 6 days leave, and if feasible I mean to have a tour on the outer circle on Saturday, so don't be surprised if I turn up.

My arm's out of a sling now, so carry on.

Yours inclusively, Syd

And sister Dorothy adds a PS: *Heaps of love and best wishes from all to all, Dor.*

Bill Withers (aged 93 in 1990) remembers Sydney's last leave. 'He was a great tall chap. Six foot of him came galloping on a mule into the farmyard at Pigeon House Farm, naval uniform three sizes too small for him'.

At the end of February 1915 Syd's parents heard that he was to be posted to an unknown destination overseas and that his troopship, the *Somali*, would sail from Avonmouth on March 1st. If they went to Avonmouth, there might be a chance to see him briefly.

It was a bitterly cold day. Ben Hall, who had been ill, stayed at home. So did sister Win, who was expecting her first child, but his mother, sister Dorothy and young cousin Ida Withers went to Avonmouth by train and gained admission to the dockyard on workmen's passes. Antony joined them later, having cycled from Fillwood. After the men, carrying full kit, had left the waiting trains and boarded the ship, Sydney appeared at the gangway with his arms full of mail which the men from his company and others had begged him to post before they sailed. Briefly united, the family spent those last few chilly hours together tearing up postage stamps and sticking them on hundreds of letters.

Sydney took leave of his family and then, without a backward glance or wave, joined the others. 'Those who look back are not fitted for the Kingdom of God', said Dorothy later. He did not reappear at the rail, although his mother and sister waited until the *Somali* steamed out at 6.30pm. They never saw him again.

On his death five months later, his papers, letters and diaries were collected together and the brief, brave sacrifice of Sydney Llewellyn Hall was unfolded to the world. War censorship did not permit members of the armed forces to give details of their movements or activities in their letters home, especially as the mission in which Sydney Hall was engaged was regarded, in its early days, as top secret. However, he had promised his family and friends that he would keep a diary and send it home when and if circumstances made it impossible for him to continue it.

Embarkation at Avonmouth

Outward bound with the s.s. Somali

<u>March 1st</u>: We left Avonmouth at 6.30pm, expecting to anchor in Kingroad for a day or two, but we went right out, accompanied by two destroyers. I went down at 8.30, and by dint of scrambling, got a hammock, and so to bed, nicely pyjama-ed, at 9.30. Cold and sickness disturbed me at midnight, and once again during the night.

<u>March 2nd</u>: Slightly sick all day. We parade at 10am, but do nothing. Feel better towards dinner time; steer SSW all day. We have 20 sentries posted to watch for submarines. Destroyers not in sight this morning. In the afternoon fire alarm (false) brings us up. Weather cloudy, but sea smoother at night. Am appointed Provost Sergeant, and see about hammock distribution. Provost Sergeant means policeman in general, head jailer and assistant tormentor. I have two other hornets [corporals] and 15 wasps [men]. No prisoners yet.

<u>March 4th</u>: Sea oily and smooth, one couldn't believe it so calm. Getting warmer too. Saw two porpoises yesterday; they followed us, jumping out of the water with great glee. Last night the sea around the ship was quite starry with phosphorescence where the water was disturbed. This ship is crowded, you should just go on the 'rounds' at night under the hammocks, they're as tight as wax together. This ship is a regular trooper, fitted up for the work, and is worked by routine in quite a good way. Hence the need for me and mine. A four-master is sailing parallel to us at about 10 miles west, probably one of our party. We should be nearly west of Spain by now, but haven't sighted land yet.

<u>March 5th</u>: Had three prisoners to lock up last night, all petty offences, but they kept me busy. Tried this morning. Hear they want me back in the section and are putting a

Sydney in uniform before leaving for Gallipoli

RMLI Sergeant on this job. Are sailing east, and expect to pass Gibraltar soon. Sea very smooth. Haven't sighted land since I saw Clevedon. Went down to see the engines this evening; good old pounders, they're giving 12 or 13 knots constantly; seems a queer thing how they keep on day and night, shoving us along.

<u>March 6th</u>: Have given up Provost Sergeant job and back to section. Last night I slept on deck in order to see Gibraltar, and about 2.30 I saw lights to port and starboard so thought we were near. We passed the rock at 6.00am this morning. Exceedingly beautiful scene in the sunlight, and the Pillars of Hercules opposite are very massive mountains, with Ceuta at the foot, little white buildings and old round houses

on the hills. A very strong east wind last night nearly blew hammock, me and all, over the stern. Also none too warm for deck sleeping. I should think this climate is about like our May for heat. The stars are all in different positions and there is little twilight here. After leaving Gibraltar we lost sight of land, and about 11 o'clock we began to see the snow-clad tops of Sierra Nevada over the clouds, about 70 miles away, I believe. We don't see anything of Africa; I suppose it's too flat.

March 7th: Last night the Sergeants organised a concert, and quite a good one, though owing to it being inside, the audience was strictly limited. Last night the wake was ablaze with phosphorescence, a gorgeous sight, and we woke this morning in full view of the Algerian coast, all mountains, presumably the Atlas range. We had a service on the fo'castle deck this morning, taken by one of our lieutenants, first time he's acted parson, I'll warrant.

It was probably about then that Sydney scribbled a note to his mother. It complied with War Office strictures to the ultimate:

Dear Mother,

I am afraid that all the items of interest which I might say won't go through, so I must limit myself to a few of them. I am well and enjoying things immensely. Was sick for a day, not badly, but since we have had marvellously smooth weather and been as right as trivets. I am keeping the diary, and will send it home as soon as I can. I have no doubt but that we are in for a very interesting time. Love to all relations. I am not writing just now as I can't say anything about things. Hope you are all well and that you got home alright last Monday.

Best and fondest love to all at Fillwood, Syd

March 9th: Sea smooth again, we are out of sight of land, but sight Malta at about 11am. Fine coast with many pronounced plateaux of volcanic origin. No grass. We reach Valetta and enter the harbour about 3pm. No shore leave. Splendid harbour with many fine houses, very densely packed. Two French cruisers in, another coming in. We find *Alnwick Castle* and the *Franconia* in harbour. Great wireless station. Much work to do. Am made Deck Sergeant to relieve Yeomans, and enter the regions internal after tea.

March 10th: Coaling all day. Crew lively. We were to sail at 7am, but haven't. 3 French submersibles came in, also one cruiser. The *Cestrian* and a French troopship also came. Valetta a fine sight, but give me an English port in preference. The natives talk Maltese, a very barbarous language. When they were coaling us, the din they made! The harbour wherries have projections on the bow and stern after the fashion of gondolas, which make them look rather smart. We left Valetta at 4.30 this afternoon and came out into a NW sea which tipped us about a bit ...

March 11th: A birthday I can remember. I remember last year when I came home from Bath [it had been his 21st]. Wasn't I tired! I also think of all the people I saw and wish them the best of health and everything. A westerly sea today, and we are sailing east, so we don't feel it. My job, Troop Deck Sergeant, keeps me down all the morning. It means foreman-housemaid, as I have to see to all the mess arrangements for 300 men. We hear that Greece has joined us in the war. All the little nations recognise Tom Tiddler's ground, and hope for gold and silver. There's not much doubt as to where we're going, it's the Dardanelles, good luck to them ...

It's the Dardanelles, good luck to them ...

Of that same day, Sydney's birthday, Sir Ian Hamilton was later to write:

Sir Ian Hamilton

On the 11th of March 1915 I was absorbed in the command of the striking force of three armies of Territorials, quartered in an irregular circle round London. On the next morning, March 12th, Lord Kitchener sent for me. I entered the room; he was writing. After a moment he looked up and said, 'We are sending a military force to support the Fleet now at the Dardanelles, and you are to have command'.

Within 24 hours I must hand over a command three times larger than the British Expeditionary Force, receive my instructions, select a staff, get the hang of the Dardanelles and of the nature and whereabouts of my new force, and bundle off ...

I had to start without any of my administrative officers, whether for supply, medicine or discipline. My troops were to be Australians and New Zealanders under Birdwood, a friend; strength say about 30,000; the 29th Division, strength say 19,000 under Hunter-Weston (a slashing man of action - an accurate theorist); the Royal Naval Division, 11,000 strong (an excellent type of officer and man under a solid Commander - Paris); a French contingent, say about a Division, under the chivalrous d'Amade. Say a grand total of about 80,000.

On the news of the appointment of Sir Ian Hamilton, Aunt Isabella couldn't resist a little name-dropping, and presently Clara had a letter from Joseph Wyatt, the gist of which she sent on to Sydney:

Another special bit of news. Sir Ian Hamilton, who is in command at the Dardanelles, is a nephew of Mrs James Caldwell of Mow, Dumbartonshire, who, before her marriage, was Miss Camilla Hamilton. Her husband, Mr James Caldwell, is Aunt Isabella's uncle, whom I have met two or three times at Kew when in my 'teens, and who used to say what a nice girl I was! Ahem!! What next shall we hear! I had a letter from Uncle Light with this news a few days ago.

The Dardanelles campaign was really the brainchild of Winston Churchill. The deadlock on the Western Front suggested to him the opening of a new battlefield in Turkey, which country had entered the war on the side of the central powers in December 1914. The capture of the Straits and Constantinople would knock Turkey out of the war, relieve hard-pressed Russian armies on the Eastern Front and bring the war to a speedy conclusion.

The Fleet bombarded the outer forts on 19th February, but the laying of mines further up the Straits and the fortification of the heights under the capable command of the German, General Liman von Sanders, meant that the Fleet alone could not now force the Dardanelles.

The news that the Royal Naval Division would form part of the army to affect a landing, gave an added urgency to the entries Sydney wrote in his diary as the s.s. *Somali* joined the convoy of troopships threading their way through the Greek archipelago.

Great rush today, getting out our webbing and equipment; we've forgotten it for a week but I bet we shall think as much about this as anything for the next month. We passed a submarine this afternoon, apparently French, though its flag couldn't be recognised.

On Friday the 13th, that ill-fated day, Sir Ian Hamilton left Charing Cross for Dover.

My staff still bear the bewildered look of men who have hurriedly been snatched from desks. An hour ago one or two of them put on uniform for the first time - leggings awry, spurs upsidedown, belts over shoulder straps! I haven't a notion of who they all are.

As the train rumbled out I missed the thrill of the step that counts. Two bad omens upset me. The first was, when dating a letter just before leaving home, I realised suddenly that it was Friday the 13th. Jean [his wife], who was bending over me, noticed the little shock and said, 'The 13th is always a lucky day for you.' But it was no use, the melancholy began to prevail over the liveliness and then, to put a topper on it, I kissed her through her veil! A gesture which in her turn, she said, was unlucky.

On that same day, s.s. *Somali* reached the rendezvous in Mudros Bay on the island of Lemnos, just over 40 miles from the Straits of Dardanelles. Sydney wrote:

Beautiful sunrise, red. At breakfast time we reached this place, the island of Lemnos, passing two destroyers, into this fine, natural harbour, which is an anchorage of about 10 sq. miles, with an entrance about 100 yards wide. We found inside the *Queen Elizabeth*, *Lord Nelson*, *Agamemnon*, *Swiftsure*, *Dublin* and a Russian cruiser, as well as about 20 transports, including the *Franconia* and *Royal George*. Fine sight. This island was Turkish and given to Greece after the Balkan War (1912), on the condition that Great Britain should use it in case of war. Cute, eh! Spent my usual hard-working day. Am getting relieved on Monday, if possible. All lights out at night.

The *Queen Elizabeth* was the flagship of Admiral de Robeck and later Sir Ian Hamilton's headquarters for the Gallipoli landings. She, the *Lord Nelson* and the *Agamemnon*, were first-class dreadnoughts and among the finest ships in the British battle fleet. Sydney reported that all three left Mudros Bay the following day (14th March). They were on their way to the massive attack on the Straits, planned for the 18th. Of the *Queen Elizabeth* he says, 'She has eight 15" guns. It should smash things up a bit'.

These were the largest guns carried by any ship afloat at that time, and on 6th March she had flung her huge shells from the Aegean Sea, right over the Gallipoli peninsula, onto the Chanak forts on the Asiatic side of the Straits. However, on that occasion, the absence of effective aircraft to direct the shells onto the target meant that the full force of these long range guns could not be wholly exploited.

Lemnos

The function of the Divisional Engineers of the Royal Naval Division was to undertake all the constructional work necessary in concentrating an army in readiness for action and, after action, to maintain communication between front line and the base. Sydney's division was soon busy preparing camp sites for the massive troop transports daily arriving in Mudros Bay.

Saturday, 14th: The Company took boats and went ashore to find a camping ground. I stayed and worked.

Sunday: The rest of the Company is getting things out of the hold. It seems we're leaving the ship. I had a party out in a boat this afternoon. Lovely day.

Monday: Ah! What a day. At 5.30 this morning we heard that we were leaving the ship at 8, and we got our equipment out and rifles and ammunition in a terrible hurry. Then we found that there was a day's work to do in getting out equipment of ropes and things onto the lighter. We managed to get away at 3 o'clock, but were only able to get within 300 yards of the shore, when we took to boats and approached to 20 yards, when we had to wade. We carried stores ashore till 8pm. Now we're slightly tired. The sea is quite warm but the bottom is rough so I wore boots, and they're wet now ...

Landing at Lemnos

Sapper Ruddock of HQ Section, which had come ashore just ahead of Sydney's company, had a camera and snapped the men wading to the beach. This and three other snaps, showing men of the RND embarking on the s.s. *Somali* in Britain, the Bay of Mudros full of warships and an encampment of tents on Lemnos, were directed by Sydney to Fillwood. His sister Dorothy wrote to him on 12th May:

My Dear Syd,

Yesterday morning we received a very pleasant surprise in the shape of four photos of the RND D.E. taken by Sapper W.B. Ruddock. They are splendid snaps and in the 'Landing at Lemnos Island' we, specially Win and I, think we can fix you. Certainly it's very like you, but we can only make out one stripe on the arm; all the same we're going to imagine it's you! I don't know how it was managed that we should get these, but whoever Sapper Ruddock may be, please thank him ever so much for us for taking the pictures.

Some weeks later Sydney confirmed this:

May 29

Yes, that's me in the Lemnos picture; golly, didn't I work that day ... and the next ... and the next ...

The camp at Lemnos with the fleet behind

Tuesday, 17th March: Started at 5am, getting the rest of the stores from the lighter ashore. Finished at 9am. Then had breakfast. We started to build a stone jetty in a rather foolish place, after our usual practice of leap before you look. We are camped on sand. I spent a fine night, last night, the sleep of the just.

Wednesday: Head Carpenter today. Making a pile-driver, a bench and all kinds of things. Bathed last night and this evening.

Thursday: More carpentering. Besides the jetty, we are making wells all over the place. Went this afternoon to get some water and took carts from Moudros, the village about a mile from here. Sandstorms this evening.

Friday: Well-digging. Horrid rain and sandstorm last night. We changed camp this afternoon to less sandy ground. Writing this in a dark tent, but have a candle now. Hear that we can get letters away tomorrow, so hope to pass one or two home. Heard that the battleships *Irresistible* and *Inflexible*, and the cruiser *Ocean*, have met trouble.

Attempt to force the Straits

The disturbing rumours which reached Sydney and his men on the 19th concerned the massive attack launched by Admiral de Robeck on the Straits the day before. The entire Battle Fleet entered the Narrows and shelled the forts at close range. The intention was to knock out the Turkish batteries and force a way through to the Sea of Marmara. The pounding of the forts went on all day and they were practically silenced when three awful explosions occurred. At 4.11pm the *Inflexible* struck a mine. Three officers and 30 men were killed and 13 wounded, and the ship began to list seriously to port. A few minutes later the *Irresistible* and the *Ocean* also struck mines and began sinking. The *Inflexible* was towed away but the other two sank, after most of their crews had been rescued.

The existence of mines in an area believed to have been cleared disconcerted de Robeck and he called off the attack. His intention was to renew it immediately the Narrows had again been cleared by trawlers, which had the unenviable task of sailing unarmed within close range of the shore batteries. However, the arrival of Sir Ian Hamilton on the eve of the battle probably convinced him that only a combined land and sea attack could force the Straits.

On the 19th of March, Sir Ian telegraphed Kitchener from Mudros Bay. 'From what I saw with my own eyes, I am being reluctantly driven to the conclusion that the Straits are not likely to be forced by battleships as at one time seemed probable. The army's part will be more than mere landings of parties to destroy forts. It must be a deliberate and progressive military operation carried out at full strength, so as to open a passage for the Navy ...'.

It was at once clear to him that such an operation could not be carried out from Lemnos which lacked the necessary resources. The troops must be sent to Egypt for training, re-sorting and re-packing in transports, ready for invasion.

Egypt

22nd March: The *Queen Elizabeth* and *Agamemnon* have come back. There is some rumour of our re-embarkation, and our stores have been partly taken on board.

23rd March: I was comfortably making a road, and Manson was carrying on his pier, when the order came to get afloat again. We got ready by 2pm. Our boats appeared about 4, and we got on board, after much waiting about in the cold, at about 9. It has been a day. We are on the *Somali* again and it is rumoured that we are going to Alexandria for concentration, as the Dardanelles aren't quite ready, and Lemnos has few resources for a large army. It's a pity we weren't allowed to stay on shore long enough to finish our job. I find five letters waiting for me, two from Dor, one from Mother, and one from Dad and one from Amy Britton. Great luck!

He replied to his parents at once:

Dear Mother and Father,

Another stage is reached. We've had a fine voyage, and I've enjoyed it very much indeed. Aren't I glad that we're not at France - this, whatever you think it is, is much pleasanter, at least I hope so. We haven't been in action yet, but we have seen signs thereof, and the other will come.

I have been working hard at domestic economy. Mess sergeant or foreman housemaid. Horrid job. I haven't come across Capt. Page yet; it will be interesting to see him. I am afraid Will's brothers are a permanent washout. I am certainly not likely to come across them.

As I can't say much about myself, I should eke out this letter with kind enquiries about all the homefolk, but can I go through the list of whom I would solicit information. No I am not writing a book, so kindly give my love to all and suitable other felicitations to sundry. Dorothy knows who sundry are - as well as most I think. My diary is assuming formidable proportions, but I can't send it on now.

Love to all, Your loving son, Syd.

4 days later - still well and enjoying myself. I find it difficult to get a letter posted. We are under canvas doing some R.E. work and so are getting a good time.

24th March: We have been expecting to leave all day; but haven't gone. I expect because we have a cook cart and water cart still on shore. When we left last night we were towed by a picket boat in ship's boats, and these aren't convenient for carrying carts, so these latter were taken by Sgt Brown, our mounted sergeant, to the jetty at Moudros, where bigger boats can come to land. But none did and the poor chap has had a night on the pier waiting. It's been a very windy day and we haven't been able to send for him; but there came along two horse boats which we are also carrying, and now he's got on board, and except for raising these boats, we're all clear. Alexandria and Port Said are the favoured butts for rumour. Have got all my clothes washed. Great joy. Heard of the fall of Prymysl today [a Polish town captured by the Germans from the Russians].

Lady Day: Got our goods stowed this morning. Got under way about 9am on a course S by E; there was quite a roll on, but it's a lovely day. Sailing through the archipelago again. I find it less exciting than one would think; although on the map the islands seem almost to touch, really they're quite a long distance apart, so that you don't often see more than two at once, and they're all similar; high, rocky and barren. I don't wonder at the old Greek mariners being such a hysterical, imaginative crowd. To be wrecked alone on one of these islands would make one see hydra, Cyclops and other fantastic horrors. Lemnos is the most fertile place we've seen since England, and goodness knows, its resources are little enough, though it would pay for cultivation. Since Greece got it after the Balkan War, they have destroyed all the mosques and built brand new churches, or vice versa to the Turks, who did just the opposite at Constantinople. I hear in their churches the custom survives of 'greeting one another with a holy kiss'. You might suggest the revival of the custom to any English parson who wants to fill his church. What ho! Wouldn't it fetch the boys and girls. Well, there's little to report about today except that there are sports coming off tomorrow, and I have entered my section for every event, including the tug-of-war, which latter I intend to win. I have a very stalwart set of men with me.

Friday: Much warmer and calmer. We passed the last of the islands at 8 this morning, steering SE. I have my men out after breakfast today, picking a tug team and gave them some coaching. There were 14 teams entered. After the usual morning roll call, we started the heats. Straight pulls being difficult, we pulled through two snatch blocks, and it gives a good test, as every pull lasts some minutes. We pulled with bare feet. We won the first two heats, and so got into the semi-final. This was settled at 4 this afternoon, when we won this and the final. The prize is £2, which we must spend when we get ashore. The other events were of little interest, and were wheelbarrow race, potato race, cock-fight, pillow fight and 'Are you there, Sambo?' This business has filled all day, so there is only time to say that the weather is as nigh perfect as the weather can be. Am sleeping on deck tonight. Our engines have a couple of loose ends, hence shaky writing.

Sydney refers to the tug-of-war contest in a letter to Dorothy that day, acknowledging the five letters he received on the 23rd:

... as regards the contents [referring to Dorothy's letter] I hope I may say that all Lill's flag-wagging was lost as we stood straight out to sea two hours after you left us. So I did not keep the tryst, for I didn't get the telegram. So sorry; and I owe Ida a letter, so must let them know how I am. Shall I write? I may, but if I don't, tell them how sorry I am, will you?

As for the letters you posted, you've no idea how grateful the fellows were for the chance to send them; you're some popular in the RND D.E. I'm glad you got home so comfortably and had such a lot of visitors and such distractions, don't you know. I note the actions of Ashton Court.

Dorothy's letter doesn't survive, but she probably informed him that since the death of Dame Emily Smyth in November 1914, her daughter and successor to the huge Ashton Court estates, Esmé Irby, had given notice that rents would be raised to pay death duties and some farms would have to be sold. Home Farm, Bishopsworth, was one.

Sydney wrote:

Is there any truth in the rumour that Uncle Arthur's retiring? [He had been the tenant of Home Farm since the death of his father, old Ben Wyatt (Clara's father) in 1867]. It seems in my recollections Mrs Irby's disease is pretty bad; have met some cases lately. [Esmé Irby (after 1914 known as the Hon. Mrs Esmé Smyth) must have given 'poor health' as the reason for running down the estate. She had phlebitis].

By the way, I don't think I've congratulated Dick on his engagement. [Richard Withers, near neighbour and old friend from Pigeon House Farm, had popped the question to Edie Snook]. I will do so, but lest I forget, do it for me, there's a good girl. He has done very well.

We haven't had any scrapping yet, and it seems to me, little though I know, that we shan't do so for some time. This

Arthur Wyatt of Home Farm

afternoon, however, we had some sports, sort of parlour games on deck, including a tug-of-war, in which, I am proud to say, that my section won first place. I found seven other 6-footers, and I tell you, what Section 1 can't do, you must take off this packet to get done. There were 14 teams besides ourselves.

I'm glad to hear Horton passes muster [Horton Hitchin was a New Zealander, enlisted in the Royal Navy] and I hope he'll have as good a time as he wishes me. Our meeting will be rapturous. The boat he came over by has had some trouble, but is alright again. Only engines, I think.

We have troops of many kinds and nations, including some Australians. There's a concert tonight, and these letters have to be done before, so I must rush off. I am quite well and fit, our company has had a week on shore, which is better than all sea-life - which is relaxing. We did some quite decent work for our keep, too. There's little more to say, except to hope everyone is well and happy, especially that Dad is better, and to send as much love as a cheap letter will carry after the censorship opens it. Your loving brother, Syd.

<u>Saturday</u>: We sighted land at breakfast time this morning, and got into Alexandria harbour at about 11am. Alexandria is a fine city; mostly European, and has a very large harbour by virtue of a breakwater, and the strip of land running out to the old forts. These are the ones battered by the *Condor*, and they haven't been touched since. What a scrap heap! We obviously came for orders, so we only anchored, and

at 4 in the afternoon we left port again. An American cruiser, the *Tennessee*, was in harbour, very spick and span, not like the *Queen Elizabeth* which, as well as our other warships, is painted in divers colours and patterns for disguise. Another big transport, *La Lorraine*, was also there from Lemnos. Don't we gallivant? Now we're sailing NE, presumably to Port Said. The coastline is quite flat here as befits a delta. We can't see the Nile, but the water is grey instead of blue as before.

Palm Sunday: Slept on deck, and got very smutty from the funnel. This, with the wind and hard deck, makes me resolve to sleep down tonight. We aren't allowed to swing hammocks on deck, because of the rounds. Steering SE this morning. We all expected to reach Port Said at midnight, but we went for some cruise or other first. We entered Port Said just after breakfast, and found it some experience. It is a small town of decidedly Eastern style, though very busy. There are two breakwaters, one very hurriedly constructed, as at Alexandria; the blocks, although cut (or moulded of concrete) to correct size, are piled together higgledy-piggledy. There are numberless ships here, including the *Franconia*, *Royal George* and *Ayrshire*. There are lots of dragonflies here, pretty big gnats, like mosquitoes, but not the real sort, I hear. We have had lots of bumboat men aboard; conjuring, diving, swindling, all sorts and sizes. Some rain today, so we haven't felt the heat. It has been rather an extraordinary Palm Sunday. I thought of the time-honoured processional at Bishopsworth.

Edwin Wyatt wrote in his diary that day: 'School and service in morning. School in afternoon. Service in evening. Fine day but cold'.

Sydney and his company spent two weeks in Egypt (29th March to 13th April). They were encamped under canvas half a mile down the Suez Canal from Port Said. The s.s. *Somali* was unloaded and cleaned, and stores, horses and fodder were transferred to bigger ships.

We hear rumours of fighting on the Canal - but nothing serious. I suppose the Turks are working this game to keep the troops in Egypt. [Egypt was still nominally under Ottoman overlordship, but their rule was only effective east of the Canal].

The work was fatiguing and hampered by sandstorms.

... there is some breeze and the sand flying is filthy. Have to keep moving not to get sanded up. Have got my sun helmet $6\frac{7}{8}$, so have had to spoil it to get it on. The sand is all over everything - doesn't it drift? Never mind, shall sleep soft and warm!

Sydney was in charge of fatigue parties, so didn't get much chance of shore leave, though he did manage to get a closer look at Port Said.

1st April: Went to town tonight - my impressions are the untidiness and dirtiness of the semi-native quarters and the pantomime effect in the well-lighted streets of the bean trees. Very pretty. Tried to enter a Greek church here, but was stopped by a man with a sword, 'No Englis - Gric'.

On Good Friday, S Section had a rehearsal for the inspection of General Hamilton, due the next day.

We had a bathe at 6am today, absolutely grand - a slight change in the usual routine for Good Friday. Stayed in tent tonight, arranging my kit.

Edwin Wyatt wrote in his almanac that day: 'Children's service. Matins. 3 hours devotion, lime-light service, evening. Wet afternoon and evening.'

<u>Saturday, 3rd April</u>: We were inspected this morning by General Hamilton; boiling hot, or hotter than that. We were congratulated on our turnout, poor though it was. But everybody's grousing at the tactless, not to say foolish, action of our O.C. in giving us a parade today. We are deemed defaulters by the rest of the camp, for it is an unwritten law - no more work after an inspection. However, I don't mind. Managed in the evening to go aboard the *Franconia* - all over her. Fine boat. Engines all silver and gold, cabins etc. great. In the first class deck houses the upholstery is very good. The walls are covered with trellis work, supporting ivy - had a most engaging effect, reminding one of a summerhouse. Well pleased.

<u>Easter Sunday</u>: Went to communion at 6am in Port Said church - a funny structure for a church, outside is all knobbly, but the sermon was good.

<u>April 6</u>: Nothing of interest except a pair of porpoises in the harbour, as big as cows. They will catch a little fish with the snap of the jaws. They travel like lightning - on their backs when after a fish. I went to see Manson who has a disease of the face and is in the Egyptian hospital, a very pretty place, like the Grand Visier's palace in the Arabian Nights. Manson is better, and will, I hope, accompany us when we leave on Thursday.

Sydney and the other sergeants got permission to use the Isolation Hospital in the ship for their quarters.

Jolly fine - but I only hope that no-one will get the mumps or fever and do us in.

<u>April 8</u>: Letters arrived from home from Mother and Dad, dated 19 March. No letter of mine home! Breakdown in postal service - shocking! Must reply to these. Our room is topping; so airy and cool.

Preparations for departure were nearly complete. The last days were spent loading hay and equipment aboard the *Ayrshire*.

<u>April 9</u>: Had a great escape. While taking a lighter of hay from the quay with a tug, we passed under the ship's cable. At this moment I was instructing some men on shore, so the cable caught me and turned me right over among the trusses. Great sport, and didn't the chaps laugh! 'It takes a sergeant to get caught like that,' said one!

On this day Clara Hall received Sydney's second letter, written from Lemnos three weeks before, in which he had gone to great lengths to be reassuring without risking security. To this totally unsatisfactory letter, Clara replied:

April 9th, 15

My dear boy, We received your <u>second</u> letter yesterday, but I assure you we were glad to get even such a little bit of news. You do not say if you have received any of our letters! We have written once - sometimes twice a week. With a rather vague address perhaps c/o GPO or Mediterranean Expeditionary Force, but it was the best we knew! The ones we sent to Walmer were evidently forwarded - as they have not been returned from the D.L.O. and I hope the others have reached you.

I know you will long for news of home, as we do of you! Winnie wrote to you from here during the week. She went home today, i.e. where she lives, but I think she <u>feels</u> more at <u>home</u> here; and certainly Will makes himself very happy here. We had cards nearly every evening - whist or bridge! ... We are invited in for the 23rd to keep up the wedding day. I wonder if you remembered *on Easter Tuesday what you were doing a year ago! I did, but no-one else seemed to think of it until I spoke of it.*

Dor and I went to see Mr & Mrs Sidney Gardiner's presents on Wednesday. [Grace Moon, the bride, daughter of the village schoolmaster, and a close family friend]. They had a good number, some of them handsome. The Gardiners and their friends gave very liberally! Vicar [Mr Ford] gave them an egg-stand. Grace looked quite pretty in her bridal dress of white crepe de chine.

John was best man - there were no bridesmaids. Mrs Gardiner was <u>not</u> at the wedding!

Dor and Son have just come home from church (Friday evening) and are having boiled rice with currants (Spotted Dick) for supper. Wouldn't you like a bit - I wonder what you give your men to eat? I can imagine domestic economy is not much in your line! I'd love to know all about what you're doing. I wish we could.

They've just brought home the news that Uncle Arthur had a huge increase in stock this morning - a cow had <u>three</u> calves - all doing well. Aunt Lizzie [Arthur's wife] has been very poorly; influenza followed by bronchial catarrh. She was at church on Sunday for the first time since her illness.

Blanche is still very keen on her Joe! I suppose this will be the next marriage! [Blanche Millier was their adopted daughter - one of the many Milliers whose father had died when they were very young and the Wyatts and their circle each took one as a kind of domestic servant. Blanche was notoriously slovenly and untidy, but she married Joe Light of Chestnut Farm in the end].

Antony, Syd's younger brother - known as 'Son'

Amy Pavey came over on Wednesday for an hour or two, but had to go back to Pilning same night - rather a long ride, eh! [bike]

Now must be off to bed. Heaps of love. Longing for the next letter, Your loving mother.

PS Jean has been very ill and is still in a nursing home. Hard luck for Mary, and Will away 'provisioning the fleet'.

The postscript about Jean, Mary and Will refers to the Page family at Westcliff-on-Sea, Essex. It was a source of great surprise and joy to Sydney, and even more to the family back home when they came to know of it, that the ship to which his section was transferred in Port Said was Captain Page's ship, the *Ayrshire*. Captain Page and his wife, Jean, were almost part of the Hall family, and how they became so is a story that reads more like fiction than fact.

Jean McCulloch was a New Zealander and the adventurous type. She worked in a small clapboard hotel in Timaru which catered mostly for seamen, and was run by Ben Hall's New Zealand cousin, Ann Webb. She was one of the daughters of Ben's aunt, Mrs Jefferis - formerly Ann Hall of Fillwood - who emigrated to New Zealand in 1858 with her husband, John Jefferis and seven children.

Ann's daughter, Mary, was a close friend of Jean, and when in 1909 Jean, who desperately wanted to see the world, accepted at short notice a vacancy as stewardess on a ship bound for Portishead, Mary wrote to Ben Hall to ask him to look out for Jean on the day of her intended arrival. On that day he and Sydney (then 14) went down to Temple Meads station in a pony and trap to meet the Portishead train. There was no sign of Jean. They stood at the barrier calling out every now and again, 'Jean McCulloch, Jean McCulloch', but to no avail.

Some hours later, Jean turned up at Fillwood Farm. There were some rather cryptic explanations about having to go to the booking office with the Captain about her ticket and when later Captain Page called to take her to the theatre, the Hall family guessed what had been going on. During the six weeks' passage from Auckland, Jean and the bachelor sea captain had fallen in love.

Jean was a sweet little thing, small-featured and vivacious and she won hearts everywhere. The Hall family took to her immediately and gave her away at her wedding, after which she and Captain Page were frequent visitors to Fillwood.

The Pages had three daughters in quick succession. Jean's illness, referred to by Clara Hall, occurred after the birth of the second child. To help with the children, Jean's old friend, Mary Webb, sailed from New Zealand and took up residence with them at Westcliff-on Sea.

As soon as Sydney knew that the *Ayrshire*, now a troopship, was part of the British convoy to Gallipoli and was in Port Said, he made every effort to visit the captain. His first attempt was foiled by red tape. 'These restrictions seem puerile, but I suppose they are necessary. Better luck next time'. Two days later he tried again. 'I went ashore this evening and made tracks for the *Ayrshire*. Found Capt. Page on the bridge and had a very pleasant couple of hours. I had dinner with him. We talked about all of you'.

On Easter Sunday, 'I went aboard the *Ayrshire* again to dinner and had a jolly evening. I learn that the two field companies are sailing in the *Ayrshire* so I hope to have a good time therein.

Next day: 'Wrote some postcards and doubled into town to post them'. They were the regulation field service postcards and subject to severe censorship.

Port Said, Mar. 5. [he should have written April].

Dear Dad,

Many thanks for hearty feelings. Am going north again on Thursday in company with Jean's husband. Hope all is well. Your loving son, Syd.

Between heavy duties and the extra fatigues he had undertaken - '... people are learning to hide when they see me coming' - Sydney got ashore once again before they sailed.

<u>Sunday 11 April</u>: What a Sunday again! I slipped my guard successfully and we went to bathe all the morning; in the afternoon took a boat, rowed to the Casino Palace Hotel, had a great tea, then got to church just in time for the benediction. Was sorry, but lost the way. The organ and singing were great and there were several English girls there. By sulphide of lime, no other can compare - for there's no such pearl as the bright and beautiful English girl. Don't wonder at the raptures; they're the first I've seen for 6 weeks ...

His family were not to read his diary for some months. All they received about Sydney's Easter was a field service postcard of extreme brevity.

On Monday 12 April his elder sister, Win, wrote to him:

My dear Syd,

I don't know if you have received any of my previous epistles as we did not know the proper address, but now we <u>do</u> know, here goes again.

I can't tell you how it altered mother getting your letter. She had got so despondent and the day after she got the letter she was as lively as a kitten. Never mind about writing to me; but whenever you can write to her, will you? Other people don't count.

We are so glad to hear that you are having such an interesting time - let's hope that you will soon be home to tell us all about it. You are seeing a bit of the world at any rate, aren't you?

Things seem to be going on just in the same old way, only poor old Willie seems to have to work harder than ever for his daily bread. However we are looking forward to a decent game of tennis in the summer, after the hard work put into the court.

I think I told you in my last letter that Jack [her brother-in-law] was in France, and so is Maurice Moon. Rather hard lines that he could not be at Grace's wedding after all, isn't it? Stanley Carpenter [son of Ben Hall's neighbours, Will and Fanny Carpenter of Tynings Farm] is a '<u>great</u> lot better', so Will heard today from Rhod [Rhodney Hall, Ben's brother]. Auntie Fan is still in London and May still housekeeper at White Cross [farm at Slimbridge]. By the way, I think Miss Lucy Withers is going to keep house for Dick [her brother] at Hart's Farm. He is not getting married yet, although we thought that would happen. Be good!!

With fondest love from Win.

On the same day Sydney wrote to his father:

Dear Dad,

Yesterday I received all the letters sent off on my birthday, so I must write to thank everyone. I heard from Mab Adams and Alfred [Pearce] besides. I was awfully pleased. I sincerely concur in all good wishes and reciprocate heartily to all the senders. Now for comments.

Glad Ma and Win had a jolly trip to Clapton. Tell them there [the Withers] their apologies for not meeting me at Avonmouth are accepted, of course. I didn't get their telegram. I hope the colt is a good goer. I enjoyed Son's [younger brother Antony] letter. Old Alf [Pearce] doesn't forget much; he's a jolly old sort. I note Dor still fetches the boys as of old. Console her for her concern about my broken heart; I lost that a long time ago, so its welfare doesn't trouble me.

Well, Dad, I've had a fine time since we came to --------, and am feeling very well and fit for a bit of strenuous work. Strange to say, we're going away again on board the 'Ayrshire', of all ships in the world.

I've seen the captain twice and had dinner with him. He didn't know me at first sight - never expected to see me at --------. Tell Jean all well and jolly. I'm sorry my letters are so few. I can't tell much, so find letters hard to write. However I think we are getting some field service postcards, so I shall shortly be able to stick one in each mail and a letter occasionally, so I propose - some proposition. Well, here's luck to us all and best love to us all. Your loving son, Syd.

To his young brother, Antony, he wrote:

Dear Son,

Just a line to let you know that I'm well and having a good time. It is possible that my next letter may be rather delayed, so I thought I must give you warning with regard to delayed letters. Captain Page tells me his letters from home are overdue, and hopes that those he sent haven't been stopped. But there's no relying on mails just now, there's so much formality to go through that they're lucky to arrive at all. I can imagine this letter and the cowslips arriving together, sincere sympathies old chap.

I have not been able to see Gough, but have written to him again. Oh, I forgot, did I tell you I had a letter from him? He heard of my whereabouts and dropped me a line some few days ago. He is <u>well</u> but seems rather fed up with his particular fate, or anyhow his enthusiasm isn't infectious.

It's likely that we shall resume our voyage today or tomorrow; so I shan't see him now, I'm afraid. Aren't you rather mystified at these continuous Channel cruises of ours? I am, but I suppose we'll arrive somewhere, some time, somehow and do something. In the meantime, keep up your pecker and be good. Give my love and tender solicitations for sobriety to all, Your loving brother, Syd.

On Tuesday 13th April the *Ayrshire* sailed. Syd wrote in his diary:

We've got nearly twice as many men as we should have, and lots of horses. So we're quite a crowd. I do hope we don't get shoved out of our billet ...

He spoke too soon:

An officer, Grierson by name, having orders to stable a submarine guard (little use they'd be) stuck them chez-nous. His real reason is apparent to us; for he'd had little toe-sucking from us, and of course, doesn't like to see us too comfortable. The ship's crowded, so what we shall do for a mess I don't know. We have permission to sleep on the boat deck, which is a concession, but what else to do, I don't know. It is a bit thick, for the sergeants' mess is a thing of great sanctity in the ordinary way.

The officers seem to have been an objectionable lot on the whole, and gave offence in other directions. Next day Sydney wrote: 'The skipper distinguished himself today by kicking one of our officers out of his chair and his chair after him ... that's what they all want, except perhaps two'.

Meanwhile, the sergeants had found a new mess - '... up for'ard, under the port quarter, and smells some', wrote Sydney. 'Next door are a lot of cabbages and they smell nasty, but it won't be bad when we've rigged it out a little'. The officers did not long enjoy their quarters. 'One of our chaps had some disease', he reported, 'which may be infectious, and he turned the late occupants, our persecutors, out of the infectious hospital - unholy glee! No land in sight today'.

But they were among the islands again on the 16th:

Very beautiful scenes, sea blue of the violet; sky grey blue; islands pink, blue, white, black. I wish I was a poet to describe it.

He contented himself by quoting Masefield:

> The sun now risen on the right, out of the sea comes he,
>
> Still hid in mist, and on the left goes down into the sea.
>
> The fair breeze blows the white foam flows,
>
> And the furrow follows free.

On 17th April sister Dor wrote from Fillwood:

My dear Syd,

You may be sure I was delighted to get your letter and PC saying that you were going north from Port Said on the 'Ayrshire'. How lucky for you to have knocked up against the captain after all; I expect both you and he were somewhat pleased, and I'm sure we are to hear of it!

Dorothy at 25 was very much the life and soul of Fillwood. She was home-loving and practical, with boundless enthusiasm and interest in people and happenings.

I expect you have heard that I went to Clapton on Monday with Phyllis.

Phyllis Wyatt, their cousin, was on a visit from York. The Withers family cousins lived in a bungalow at Clapton called 'Glenmere' and were regularly visited, particularly as one of their daughters, Ruth, was Sydney's goddaughter. 'Fido', the mother, was, before her marriage, Lily Britton, daughter of Clara's sister, Sarah.

Now, of course, you'll be wanting news of your little 'responsibility' at Glenmere! Well, that's a very sweet little kiddie, but I tremble to think of her form of speech in the future, as she certainly will get to talk as the others do - and thern' no descriptive word for <u>that</u>! After having been told who I was, she called me 'God Mammy' all the time and when Fido said, 'Where's God Pappy?' she said at once, 'In a boat', so you see, she quite realises who you are and all about you.

While there, I converted one of Dorothy's old hats into a bonnet for Ruth, and though young, she already has a spark of vanity visible as the 'pitty new ha-ta' took a prominent part in her thoughts and conversation afterwards! Still, as I said before, she is a darling! All the Glenmere folk are well and Fido says she will write to you in a day or two.

Dorothy ('Dor'), Syd's sister

I don't know when Edie will take up the management of Dick and his 'Harts' [Harts Farm], but I have an idea it won't be a very distant time as his idea of a carter and his wife in the house doesn't seem likely to become a reality - such a couple doesn't seem to be wanting the place. At present Lucy [Lucy Withers, Dick's sister] is trying her skill as a housekeeper with a young woman to do the <u>extra</u> every day and the young woman's mother to help her occasionally. I called there this afternoon and found everything going swimmingly, but Lucy does not intend staying more than 2 or 3 weeks, as she thinks the young woman will be able to do after ...

John Britton [their cousin, Highridge Farm, Bishopsworth] has had £10 knocked off his rent, on appeal, so that's rather better.

Highridge Farm, like Fillwood, was rented from Lord Temple, and twice a year the farmers rode over to Newton Park, near Bath, to pay the rent, where they were treated to the customary dinner and ale and came home more often than not a little tipsy, and content on the whole that Lord Temple was their landlord. The farmers were not to know it but the Temple estate, like most large estates, was on the verge of bankruptcy, and the war precipitated a general sale of farm land.

I expect Mother has told you that Alfred was up last weekend, looking terribly white and thin, but jollier than he's been for ages.

Alfred Pearce, a former colleague of Sydney, who lived in Carrington Road, Bedminster, was at that time generally considered to be Dorothy's young man, but the courtship was in the doldrums, owing partly to Alfred's poor health, and partly to the war. His brother, Harold, had already joined up and was fighting on the Western Front, and Alfred desperately wanted his commission in the Navy.

He is working very hard, and the course is being pushed through at lightning speed. He writes that there will be no more exams until the final, so it's likely that will be fairly soon; certainly not two years distant.

We have not heard news of Stanley [Carpenter] since Tuesday; he does not get on very quickly though up to then was improving slowly.

We were glad to hear that doctor and nurses pronounced Auntie a little better this week. [Sarah Britton, Clara Hall's eldest sister, was mentally ill and was being treated at Doctor Fox's famous institution at Brislington].

Friday is the Evans' wedding anniversary, so Mother and Dad are having a night off [presumably driving the trap over to Belluton Road, leaving Dorothy to hold the fort at Fillwood. Of course, the war was the main talking point, especially the Mediterranean Expeditionary Force and its yet unknown destination].

Such lots of transports go out from and into Avonmouth on every tide, and yesterday from 8am until 3pm on and off, the guns at Portishead and Avonmouth were being fired for practice, and the horses waiting to go to the front were kept near, to be broken in. There seems to be quite a lot of soldiers about yet.

Heaps of love from all; especially your loving sister, Dor.

That day, Sydney awoke to find a destroyer trailing them, for there was fear of a Turkish night attack. Captain Page had his eyes skinned for torpedo boats and a lighter, which had slipped its cable from the *Alnwick Castle*, and consequently showed no control signals, gave them all a fright.

Early on the 18th, 'A wondrously fair morning', they were back in Lemnos harbour.

It felt quite homely - what a sensation for such a place! There are lots of battleships - the *Queen Bess, Agamemnon, Lord Nelson, London, Prince of Wales, Implacable, Dublin* and a few more; besides several French boats, which one cannot, by any repression, fail to ridicule. They are most ridiculous. Let's hope they can fight.

Events were evidently moving to a climax. The great invasion at six points along a 20-mile stretch of coast on the Turkish mainland was only hours away. The sight of the world's greatest navy afloat - coal burning, their towering superstructures trailing black smoke across the Aegean Sea - must have been sublime.

There are more transports than I can tell, with British, French and Australians aboard, to say nothing of the R.N.O. Probably 50,000 men. Spent most of the day mending electrical instruments, mine are not very good ones so I'm trying to improve them.

After that, there wasn't much to do. The sergeants had regained their mess in the old infectious hospital, '... so will be luxurious again'. They played cards and waited. Sir Ian Hamilton, aboard the *Elizabeth*, was waiting for favourable weather for the 21st was a rough, rainy day.

HMS Queen Elizabeth

22nd: I had two letters today, one from Dor, one from Win. Referred to Stanley being 'better' in London, and a letter from Mother which hasn't arrived. I suppose I haven't heard about the first, because I haven't got the second.

Sir Ian Hamilton planned the attack for the 23rd April - St George's Day - but the weather was still unsettled, so it was postponed for 24 hours, and then a further 24 hours.

23rd: Nice calm weather; we're expecting movement soon. We hear that a ship here, the *River Clyde*, has holes in her side for landing parties to go through after they've beached her. Quite a scheme. Reminds me of the horse of Troy, and Troy is very near here. I said there weren't many troopships here, but on further examination I find there are about 50. They are marked B (British Regular); A (Australian); N (Naval Division); S (Supply Ships) and H (Headquarters). Also about 10 battleships and several cruisers and torpedo boats. The *Queen Eliz.* is still here, looking like a great floating fort.

Dear Win,

It's very fitting that today, the anniversary of your wedding, I should write to you, and I find it the less difficult because I have something to say. It is that the past year having been a test in many ways of many people of our circle, I hope and trust that in all future years they may reap the reward of their steadfastness in quiet and joyful living. This is a general statement, particular applications you can make. Specially, however, I wish you and Will all the happiness that your amiability and unselfishness deserve.

Well, Win, there have been some goings-on at home! Grace and Sidney I wish all joy and prosperity. He deserves <u>all he gets</u>. I know him and believe him to be the victim of cruel fate in his career. I hope his last stroke will turn Fortune into a high speed reversible engine and chuck the link over quick.

... I note the distinctions of the boys [Jack Evans and Maurice Moon in France], and I may say I think I've struck oil compared with their 'bilgy fillets'. In particular, I wonder what's wrong with Stanley. Dor refers to his being better, but I have no news of his illness. Wounds or meningitis? I hope not the latter; it isn't at all nice as we know from experience.

I note from Dor that George Snook has been back, 16 stone, is he? Scarred too! He should be a man to be proud of; also of what Alfred is doing; now's the time, and good luck to him. He'd like to be here though, I know. Specially the next few days which I expect will contain some of the most wonderful sights and experiences of my life. This place looks too placid; even a score of battleships don't make it look fit for its destiny. You can box the colour compass at a glance; blue below, white ashore, green slopes, red hills, purple mountains, grey horizon to deep blue heaven. It's a glorious day.

I may now say that I am well and enjoying myself. We sergeants roll in the luxurious ease in what was the infectious hospital, now happily vacant of patients. It now approaches 9am when you and I will think of one thing only. Only to synchronise, I must call 12, 9. [Win was married at 9am, 23rd March 1914].

To conclude, give my best to all friends and relations, not forgetting a little girl [his god-daughter, Ruth] whose picture, among others, adorns the wall of this room, the sergeants' art gallery; and tell her that, by an important judge, she gained 1st prize. That's rather cryptic, eh? Naval Reserve.

It's time for me to take a physical drill class, so adieu all who care, Yours ever, Syd.

Signals that the landings would take place on the 25th were relayed to the Fleet by Admiral de Robeck, and from their bases round the Greek islands of Tenedos and Lemnos the transports converged on the Dardanelles. Sydney reported that nearly all had left Lemnos by the 24th, 'It seems there will be something doing soon'.

As the function of the Royal Naval Division was to give support to the regulars once a landing was made, Sydney did not take part in the great battles of the 25th, and was one of the last to leave, much to the fury of his men, who could hear the crashing of the guns, but could see and do nothing.

26th, Monday: Severe grousing about our fate today. Much firing heard and we hear rumours of a landing being effected by the regulars. We don't hear much, I expect you hear more. The inaction is not really unpleasant, but we would like to see things. The operations must be unique in interest, even to see. Have played any amount of auction bridge lately. I can imagine people at home thinking hardships. Quaint notion.

One who did see the departure from Mudros Bay was John Masefield with the Red Cross, and he described in his faultless prose how the ships, '... moved out of harbour in the lovely day; and felt again the heave of the sea. Their feeling that they have done with life and were going out to something new, welled up in those battalions; they cheered and cheered till the harbour rang with cheering. As each ship crammed with soldiers drew near the battleships, the men swung their caps and cheered again, and the sailors answered and the noise of cheering swelled, and the men in the ships not yet moving joined in, and the men ashore, till all life in the harbour was giving thanks that it could go to death rejoicing. All was beautiful in that gladness of men about to die, but the moving thing was the greatness of their generous hearts. As they passed the French ships, the memory of old quarrels healed, and the sense of what sacred France had done and endured in this great war ... and they cheered the French ships more even than their own'.

On one transport was displayed an enormous canvas screen on which was painted in bold lettering, 'TO CONSTANTINOPLE AND THE HAREM'.

The elation of that momentous hour comes across in the last two entries in Sydney's diary.

Tues. 27th: Now we've got a move. The morning was as usual somewhat somnolent, but early this afternoon we got orders to proceed to Tenedos, and to be ready for eventualities. We had full marching order parades and issued more ammunition and iron rations. I also looked after my tool cart - getting it ready to land.

Tonight we're right in the mouth of the Dardanelles, and I've seen my first shot of the real thing, for the boats here are still bombarding the land behind Seddülbahir with shrapnel some 3 or 4 miles away. We are against the *Franconia* and the *Queen Bess* is just by us, as well as the *Agamemnon*, who has had her bridge blown away. I am intending to give this account of my adventures to the skipper to send home; I don't think I need to tonight, there's another day tomorrow.

Wednesday morning: I said so! Well, the bombardment has been resumed this morning; it seems the point of Gallipoli is cleared and the rest is clearing, so we are succeeding. The guns are making a great row, especially those of the *Implacable* which is only 2 miles from us. The great ship about 400 yards away is not the *Queen Elizabeth* but the *Warspite*, so it seems that England is getting these big boats out very fast, long before they were expected, and I think now Britannia will always rule the waves. I don't know when we are going ashore, but I expect it will be on the Asiatic side, south of Kum Kale, where I hear some of the R.N.D. are gone.

However, I must close this diary and give it to the Captain. as if we get landing orders, there will be no time or chance. So I say, I shall go high-spirited; for are we not succeeding, and long may England succeed.

I thank God for my country, relatives, friends, and past life, and pray for his mercy and blessing on all. Adieu, all who read, Syd.

His sentiments were echoes by the C.O., Sir Ian Hamilton, who wrote that night in his diary:

Almighty God, Watchman of the Milky Way, Shepherd of the Golden Stars, have mercy on us ... Thy will be done. En avant ... at all costs ... en avant!

The story of those heroic landings, the fearful carnage, the sea running with blood as wave upon wave of men waded ashore, sometimes on the fallen bodies of their comrades, wrestled with barbed wire and were decimated by machine gun fire from clifftop positions which the Turks - under the direction of the veteran von Sanders - had had four months to prepare, are part of our imperial history, and need no repetition here.

Seddülbahir fort and village seen from the beached British troop carrier s.s. River Clyde on the morning of 25 April 1915 during the landing at Cape Helles. The black mass huddled on the beach in the middle of the photograph is a group of British soldiers who had just landed from the troopship and were pinned down by Turkish machine gunners located in the fort. The lighter in the foreground contains dead from the Royal Munster Fusiliers and The Hampshire Regiment who were killed while attempting to get ashore.

On the evening of the landings, Clara Hall wrote to her son:

Fillwood, Bishopsworth, Sunday evening, 25.4.15.

My dear boy,

I have been studying the map and wondering if you are one of the party to land at Enos last week, and what is happening. Naturally we look out for news from the Dardanelles every morning, but tis little we learn up to now! I am sending you last Saturday's paper with some bits marked. Our many friends are now in France. Maurice [Moon] is stretcher-bearer, but has had no cases up to now, so Mrs Moon told me this morning. [It was generally believed by the Hall family that Maurice had plumped for a soft option and, when later he was transferred to a regimental band whose functions were merely ceremonial, their opinions were confirmed].

In church [where evidently everything was not entirely to Mrs Hall's liking], the organ is under repair. Part of it was propped against the wall of the church, all the top pipes out, so we had the extreme pleasure of an American organ to accompany the choir this morning and I do so dislike this form of music! Still I suppose it is better than nothing.

Dear Mr Taylor was there - asked very kindly after you - of course, he would! He has not given us the pleasure of seeing him lately ...

It is so cold this afternoon we have a huge fire to sit by. Dad and I are alone. Dor and Antony gone to church. I rather thought Win and Will would have come over this evening, but I expect it was a bit too rough for Win. Dad and I were in Knowle on Friday to keep up the wedding day. Will was in good spirits, having had a rise of £20 during the week. [He was mailing clerk for John Robinson, an animal foodstuffs company at Redcliffe. His father had been station master at Temple Meads, but Will never rose much further than forwarding clerk].

Everything has gone up in price so much, I doubt if he'll find it goes farther. On Friday I went into town again and visited Mr Dunscombe and as a result I am now wearing new glasses which I bought as a present from you - so I hope now to be able to read or sew in the evenings comfortably!

We were interested to find you were in the 'Ayrshire'! I had a letter from Jean yesterday. She has returned to White Heather and has only to make haste to get strong, she says. She had heard from the Capt. since he met you and says you were looking splendid! Mary [Webb] has been a brick, to do all she has had to do when Jean was so ill. No doubt she is most capable and loving.

Belle Flowers' banns published for third time today [Inyn's Court Farm] and not forbidden, so I suppose we must expect a wedding there to a Mr Stevens of Stanton Drew! And nobody seemed to have heard a sound about it until the banns were called!

Longing to get another letter from you. Heaps of love from Dad and Mother.

Across the top of the letter she wrote and underlined: *Good luck to the R.N.D.D.E.*

Dorothy wrote briefly next day, full of consternation about Alfred Pearce:

I had a letter saying that he was not feeling well, so on Thursday last, saw the doctor who promptly ordered him to bed, where he has been ever since, feeding on nothing but milk! He says he does not know what's up with him and the doctor seems a bit puzzled, but I think I know the cause - overwork with not enough rest or food. In his letter he said he hoped to be about today, as he would have a week's instructions to make up then, but I don't think so, if he was having nothing but milk up to Saturday. I do hope this won't stop him passing for Warrant Officer, as I know it would be a terrible disappointment. Rotten luck, isn't it?

Can't stop for more now, Heaps of love, Dor.

And from Belluton Road, the same day, eldest sister Win put pen to paper, evidently with difficulty:

I feel so ashamed, for I know how you must like letters now. We think of you ever so much, and Mother sends all your letters over to us to read, so we know all there is to know - but that isn't much, is it.

There followed banalities about the weather and the wedding anniversary etc. and then:

Last year this time Hilda Lucas brought round a lovely bowl of lilac to greet us on our return [from honeymoon - a weekend in London]. But this year the leaves are just shooting, so it shows what a lot of cold weather we have had.

Win was now six months pregnant, but the birth of twins to a neighbour did not elicit particularly maternal feelings:

I have been across the road to see the twins. I suppose they are both nice babies, but I don't know much about such things, I'm afraid.

I'm nearly asleep, so will stop now. I will try to write again in a few days. Hoping to see your smiling face again soon ...

Will was prevailed upon to fill up the rest of the page - full of apologies for not having written before and rather stiffly:

No doubt you know we are expecting a family end of June. Do hope we shall not follow the people opposite - it would be awful to have twins to start off with, eh?

I heard from Jack last week. He said he had had a shot at the Germans. It looks pretty bad over there just now, don't you think so? Have just been hay-making in back garden, so in consequence feel rather tired. We shall both be very pleased to hear from you when you have time. With fondest love and best of luck, Willie.

On the 27th April desperate battles were raging along the clifftops as the shattered remnants of landing parties struggled to link up and dig themselves in. By the 28th, the Turks were dislodged from their positions and a precarious hold on the southern tip of the peninsula was made. Despite utter weariness and appalling casualties, Sir Ian Hamilton ordered a further advance while the Turks were still disorganised, and to give more security for the landing of stores and guns.

Sydney's first day ashore, 28th April, was the day of the so-called First Battle of Krithia. With extraordinary tenacity, the allied forces of England and France (the French still wore blue tunics and red trousers, as they did in the Franco-Prussian War of 1870), with fixed bayonets, drums and bugles and a deafening cannonade from the big ships out to sea, pushed forward across the scrubby plateau. By midday the advance ground to a halt and clung to a line across the peninsula about a mile from Cape Helles.

Meanwhile, the Anzacs (Australian and New Zealand Army Corps), under Colonel Birdwood, had been put down 12 miles up the Aegean coast. It was intended to be a surprise night attack to coincide with the landings at Cape Helles, but the Turks spotted the landing buoys, shifted them a mile further north and so, instead of landing in a gap in the cliffs at Gaba Tepe, the Anzacs were confronted with almost vertical cliffs 600 feet high at Ari Burnu. Though every nook and cranny was crammed with Turks, the Anzacs winkled them out, one by one, and gained the clifftop in one of the most heroic actions of any war.

Sydney's movements after 28th April 1915 only later came to light. On going ashore, he had closed his diary and given it to Captain Page to take home and from then on his family could only guess from intermittent letters his personal experience of the action, and he deliberately didn't tell them everything.

Much more information survives in his pocket book which came back to his family after his death, but as the entries were not consecutive, had been made in pencil which had faded so much as to be scarcely legible, and were mixed with a great deal of other data (lists of names of the men in his section - their trades, duties, sick parades, fatigues and jargon, including international flag signals, phrases for addressing Turkish prisoners etc.), his family could make little of them.

In 1978 the pocket book was loaned to the Malago Society and it was subjected to detailed scrutiny. It had hard cloth covers, much stained and worn at the edges from being pushed in and out of his pocket. On the cover was written 'Sgt SL Hall, Section 1, 1st Field Coy D.E. R.N.D.' The pages were the usual War Office regulation squared leaves, many of which had been torn out for letters, messages etc. when there was no other paper to hand. On the inside front cover he had written, 'In the event of my death, please forward this book and the contents of my pockets to Mr B. Hall, Fillwood, Bishopsworth, Bristol, England'.

Each small faded page was examined through a magnifying glass, deciphered, copied and eventually typed. Only then could the personal details be separated from the official memoranda.

It began on April 15th, nearly two weeks before the landing, and so overlaps with the diary. But the lists of men on submarine guard, on sick parade, oat crushing, potatoes or hay loading, hatchway cleaning fatigues etc. is occasionally supplemented by personal observations, sometimes flippant or subjective, depending on how the mood took him.

'Sapper May (in civvy street, a labourer) on Submarine Guard, did not turn up, owing to being on table 13', he wrote on April 15th. The roll call shows he did turn up for guard on the 16th, and on Sunday 18th he was put on latrine fatigues - probably as a punishment.

After 28th April, the personal jottings become more frequent, though they did not accompany the lists of guard duties, church parades and increasing numbers of sick and wounded. They were written at the back, but as each entry was scrupulously dated, the personal comments can be linked to the official state of his section, and so an intimate picture emerges of those three vital, hectic and final months of his life.

For Wednesday 28th, the day of his landing, he wrote: 'Closed diary. Left Seddülbahir for Gaba Tepe 11am. False preparation to land due to reconnaissance aeroplane report of deserted battery'. So his section was not sent to the Asiatic side, as he had thought, but to the eastern tip of Cape Helles, to the little beach where the *River Clyde* had discharged her human load into underwater barbed wire and murderous machine guns three days before. The old Turkish fort and village of Seddülbahir had been stormed and taken that day and when Sydney arrived, a causeway was being hastily constructed to enable big guns to come ashore and ammunition and supplies were being stored in the fort.

His section (Section 1) were not, at first, involved in this operation:

After hanging about for two days, we landed at Gaba Tepe and stayed there a day making a gun road for the Australians, whose engineers had become disorganised [from a letter to his father, July 8th]. This was only a fill time job and we had to join our Division immediately, so we re-embarked [much to Capt. Page's disgust; he had probably had more than he could stomach from Army officers] and went to Cape Helles and landed at Seddülbahir, and we've been hammering away at this job ever since, our work, since a definite line was established, being communication trench digging and maintenance, assisting in advances and construction of new line trenches. A very monotonous job in a blazing climate, is what our scientific, well-educated youths are come to; and it's pulled some of them about ...

<u>Thurs. 29 April</u>. Bombardment of Hill 971 by *Swiftsure*, *Doris* and *Majestic*. Maidos bombarded by *Swiftsure*.

<u>Fri. 30 April</u>. Reveille 5am. Making rounds for guns till 7pm. Re-embark 1am tomorrow. Escape from Shrapnel. Fine sight indeed at evening.

<u>Sat. 1 May</u>. Wrote home. Resting on board. Bombardment severe tonight. Presented Capt. with shell head. 'Am I an ass? No'.

At any rate, Capt. Page brought the shell head, with its marking in Turkish, back to Fillwood, where, its brass finely polished, it did duty for many years as a paperweight in the Hall family.

The letter he wrote home that day survives:

May 1st

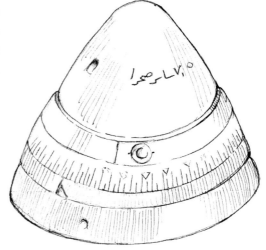

Had a letter of yours, and one of Win's today. I'm in luck, for most of the chaps didn't get anything. So you weren't sure of the address before my 2nd letter came, eh? Well it was near enough, but perhaps they'll come quicker from Charing X. I note all the news, and certainly remember last year's doing on Easter Tuesday, and such times - quite eventful. Am on board today, getting over yesterday's strenuous effort when we were on shore doing a job. Have been asleep all day - and very satisfied and happy. It's great fun and so interesting here; I never thought to have such a good time. Am glad Stanley's such a great lot better ... (to quote Roddy - could tell that kiddie's patter anywhere).

Have met Indians and Australian troops and they're jolly good; especially the latter. Well this letter is only a reminder to keep the pot boiling, so hoping all are well and keeping 'yatt'. Best and fondest love to all, Syd.

On 29th April, 1st May and 2nd May, Dorothy, Clara Hall and young brother Antony wrote to Sydney. By now the Dardanelles landings were in the headlines.

Dor: *We see by the papers that troops have landed at Enos and other places near the Dardanelles, and have had some hard fighting already. Apparently with some success, may it be the fore-runner of speedy and complete success!*

Mother: *No letter from you since I wrote last. We quite expect you landed about last Sunday 28, so we are hoping to get a line during the week.*

The main item of news related by all three was the night operation carried out by a unit of Bristol University's O.T.C. (Officer Training Corps) on 30th April/1st May. Mrs Hall even sent Sydney two typed sheets of their scheme. In the 'General Idea' the position is outlined thus:

'An advanced Guard (of all arms - including two battalions of infantry) of a Blue invading column marching west, has met and driven back the advanced troops of a Red force which is in position to the east of Bishopsworth. The Advanced Guard has made good, and is holding, at noon of the 30th April, the position Redcatch Lane, Queen's Dale Farm, Open Air School.

'The chief incident of the afternoon of Apr. 30 has been an attack by half a battalion (Blue) from the direction of Queen's Dale Farm, which, however, was not pushed further than 150 yards west of Hengrove House.'

Night marching orders for the Blue invading force was 'to advance during the night of April 30/May 1 and to capture Fillwood Farm at dawn, as a preliminary to the general attack. Another Coy. has been detailed to attack Novers Hospital ... operation will commence at 10.30pm on April 30 at Queen's Dale Farm'.

Dor: *This morning (29 April) Lieut McBain and two other 'somebodies in khaki', motored over and made arrangements to bring the O.T.C. over here tomorrow night ... They warn us not to be afraid of the firing as they'll be using blank cartridges. They are coming to make final plans tomorrow afternoon. Tomorrow is Guild Night (Intercession Service at 8pm and Guild after) so Antony and I will be coming home about the time of their arrival, I expect, so don't be surprised to hear that we are taken for spies.*

Mrs Hall had more to say about the other 'somebodies in khaki':

We had Lieut McBain, Sgt James and Private Cope-Proctor here to tea on the 30th. The latter a 'batman', but owner of a lovely little 2-seater car! [Motor cars were still a rarity in rural places]. He is nephew of the late Thomas Proctor, the well-known chemical manure manufacturer. We were surprised to find how nervous Lieut McBain was in company.

No wonder - having his Private's credentials, not to mention his two-seater car, paraded in public! Clara Hall could be rather formidable when it came to name-dropping and in this particular 'company' had probably also trotted out her connections with Sir Ian Hamilton - very much the man of the hour - to poor Lieut McBain's further embarrassment.

Antony's letter was full of teenage jargon and attitudes of the age:

Dear Syd,

Here it is at last (the long expected I should think). Why is it I haven't written before? Because I've been too thundering lazy, that's it exactly. Well, now I've started I'll 'carry on', or try to. I haven't got much news so I must put in what little I have. I went to Winford sale on Tuesday to see what my lambs are worth, and incidentally (is that spelt right?) to pick up any knowledge there was lying about. Well the biggest of my lambs is worth about 42/- I should think.

On the way home I went into Castle Farm. What for? To see auntie, of course. [Hester Elizabeth Froud, wife of Alfred, was Ben Hall's sister]. No-one else? S-s-s-certainly not; nothin' doin' there. F.K. is not the wench for me. Was' think thou? Will Needham's banns were called this a-m, I don't know the girl (a Miss Butcher from the Queen's Head in 'Little Hell', 'the Barracks' or 'Upper Village', whichever you like) [now Withywood].

By the way, I forgot to say (not rhyme) that as I was coming home on Tues. I went in at 'The Corner' to see how the old man was (I suppose you have heard that 'D.R.' [Dorothy Russell] has been cooking so badly lately that she has given him dis-pep-si-a). Anyhow, he has got so far behind the market that he offered me some tegs and lambs at about 10/-, a couple less than their value!!!!!! But what thundering use is that when you're stony broke? He then asked me to buy two pigs. I asked him if he meant the two girls, and suddenly I got from somewhere a clout across the head, and a box on the ear to keep it company.

Turning round, I saw a graceful form disappear through the door, but I managed to avoid tumbling over any coal-box for the form soon reappeared with a grin on its face. I suppose you have heard I am breaking in Uncle Arthur's Dolly [Arthur Wyatt of Home Farm, Clara's brother], but in case you've not, I am, but I'm 'taking et yasy', only getting on her back when I feel like it; but the tennis court is fenced in now, so I must get on with it, I suppose.

I hear that Dick and Lousy are coming up on Tuesday (this is to make you envy me, I don't think). I expect you have heard that all our ground (bar 7 acres) is cropped. Don't you think my writing has improved since I left school? I do. We had the O.T.C. of the Univ. here Friday night and although they fired about 300 rounds we none of us heard a sound until one of the sergeants blew his whistle just outside my window and called out to say that they had selected me as May Queen, you will see from this that I didn't stay up to see the fun but according to Lieut McBain it was very tame, as the attackers only attacked a couple of rifle pits in Murphy's ground instead of coming on into their grand barb wire entanglements and tearing their clothes whilst they were shot at, so I'm not at all sorry I didn't stay up.

My stock of news, lies and rot is entirely exhausted for the present - soooooo ta ta. Good luck and brotherly love to thee, from your fool of a brother, A.D.H.

Mrs Hall finishes the story:

The O.T.C. Cadets had their coffee about four in the yard behind the barn. The cook boiled it where the cricketers have their water boiled for tea! I dare say they enjoyed it, but were very tired. Isabella Flower was married on Wed. Very quietly, I expect.

Dorothy had quite a bit more about Dick and 'Lousy' as Antony terms her.

On Tuesday last when going to post, Lucy saw me and hauled me into Hart's Farm to tea [next to Parson Street station - Willada Close now occupies the site]. Dick was off to see his beloved just as soon as tea was over; so of course I 'pulled his leg' a bit! He and his housekeeper are coming up here for the evening next Monday. It is quite a treat to be able to <u>enjoy</u> Dick's company! I am everlastingly indebted to Edie; only hope it won't be long before she takes up her abode in Parson Street.

Coming home from Parson Street, Dor called in at Locks Mills to see her great friend, Miss Hall, and her mother, only to find the old house full of relations; a grandmother and younger brother.

I was in a fearful hurry to get home. It was really as Auntie Alice [Brook Farm, Bishopsworth] was here, but I was not to be let off, I <u>had</u> to see them and after all they weren't much to be afraid of ... I'm still alive!

Most of her letter was devoted to the unsatisfactory Alfred Pearce.

You will be sorry to hear that old Alfred is still having enforced rest. I had a letter this morning, written from the R.N. Hospital where he has been since Sat. and even now it is not known what is the matter. He says he never felt better in his life, but the doctors maul him about every morning and have X-rayed his chest and still don't know what's wrong, but they are keeping him under close observation for something! He takes no medicine, but three times a day the '<u>Angelic Sister</u>' presents him with a tablespoonful of Virol [a branded vitamin preparation based on malt extract] and he has the appetite of two wolves! I hope they won't find what they expect, for certainly that is something not very desirable. I'm afraid the cocked hat will be a long time finding its way to his head now! Worse luck!! [the 'cocked hat' being the naval officer's hat which would come with his hoped-for commission].

Both Mrs Hall and Dor were more than usually solicitous about Sydney's needs now that he was in action. Dor wrote:

Last Thursday afternoon I posted a tin box full of sweets to you; hope you will get them alright. Mother thought I had better take the parcel to post instead of trusting it to Alf [Alfred Pitman, a farm labourer], so I cycled down and was very much surprised to find how little it cost to send with your new address - only 5d. - and it was quite a heavy parcel! We shall certainly try again.

Dad has gone to town today and back to Belluton Road to meet mother who went over this afternoon and I expect they'll soon be back, so must light the fire (past 8 o'clock) and get supper.

How are you faring in the way of necessities - food and clothing? asks his mother. *Is there anything I can send you? Socks or anything. If so, do tell me. Have you received the chocs? Hoping you are keeping fit and well and that we shall have good news of you.*

Alfred Pitman, farm-worker at Fillwood

Do send a card as often as you can. We long for news. Heaps of love from us all and best wishes to you and success to the R.N.D. from your loving mother. Dad is fairly well and sends his love to you.

Mrs Hall's postscript had a delightful period flavour:

P.S. Oh! Miss Chapman that was, is going with her husband to India on S.P.G. work, leaving England in Oct. Chata Nagpur.

Miss Chapman was one of Sydney's earlier 'flames'.

<u>Sunday May 2nd</u>: Disembarked 9am. Landed at Seddülbahir after a cruise on yacht because anchor fouled. 1 shrapnel shell near. Pitched bivouac. Afternoon - making road on W Beach.

W Beach was a break in the cliffs at the extreme southern tip of the peninsula, midway between Cape Helles and Tekke Burna. Here a gully opened out into a small bay with a curving beach and gentle sand dunes a quarter of a mile across. In an epic action six days before, 630 out of 932 men of the Lancashire Fusiliers had fallen storming the Turkish barbed wire entanglements and gun positions in the cliffs on either side. Only 17 out of 80 naval ratings, who had manned the cutters and tows, escaped death or injury and half of the officers were killed. But the heights had been cleared by the bayonet and now it was vital to pull up the big guns.

<u>Monday May 3rd</u>: Making redoubt about X Beach. Very quiet day. 4 companies of Sikhs are working parties for Sect. 1.

X Beach is half a mile round the headland and faces west across the Aegean. Here, on the 25th, 750 Royal Fusiliers made a model landing, with the shells from *HMS Implacable* blasting the top of the cliffs above them, and the Turkish guns with them, to atoms.

<u>Tues. May 4th</u>: Continuing redoubt by ourselves. 2 aeroplane bombs dropped at *Swiftsure*. Spent the night in 2nd line trenches in case of attack.

<u>Wed. May 5th</u>: Back at camp. Rested all morning. Wired redoubt. Some shrapnel. Rations served late for early morning start.

Orders had already been given for what was subsequently known as the Second Battle of Krithia. Sir Ian Hamilton decided that a fresh push forward was imperative before Turkish reinforcements could consolidate their new positions across the southern slopes of Achi Baba - a 200-foot high outcrop about two miles to the north. The land between Achi Baba and the allied landings was a rolling plateau - somewhat depressed in the middle, like a saucer. In a letter to his father (May 22nd) Sydney wrote:

This country is of an undulating nature, with streams in the nullahs or hollows, and the slopes are clothed mostly with scrub consisting of a kind or rock rose and holly-like shrub (dwarf), also some thorn. There are some Scotch firs and a few small larches, also olives and kinds of willow, ash and oak, but not the English varieties. The country is roughly cultivated; the soil being of a sand and clay structure. Undoubtedly a beautiful place, more like home than anywhere else I've been.

Then, as now, the cultivated patches blended naturally with the pieces of woodland, and fields of corn, cotton and sunflowers, strewn with olives and wild pear, formed a picturesque kaleidoscope. With the refreshing breeze from sea to sea, the turquoise ocean ever visible, the wild flowers in spring and its extreme isolation, the beauty of this place beguiles all who see it for the first time. The Gallipoli peninsula, sprinkled with war cemeteries, is now designated a national park.

From the military point of view it offered no advantage. Allied troops had no natural protection from the batteries in front of Achi Baba, or the big guns pounding the peninsula from Kum Kale on the Asiatic side of the Dardanelles. After a preliminary bombardment of half an hour from the Fleet, the attack opened at 11.30am and continued intermittently for the next three days.

Extraordinary courage was displayed by the 29th Division, many of whom were from India and Egypt, but the frontal assault by first, second and third lines in long uncontrollable charges against unreconnoitred positions and with invisible objectives, was predictably futile. The first line was decimated and in some places the second also. It was Sydney's first actual battle and his experience is typical:

Thursday May 6th: Set out at 3.30am. Spent all day in sandy trenches. Lieut Marshall wounded crossing in single file under shrapnel. Spicer killed, Fry wounded. Fooled about all night trying to find Drake lines. Counterattack by Turks. Advanced 2,000 yards today. Jones wounded. When we retired slept in trench.

Friday May 7th: Rested after proceeding to base till 4pm. Set out and occupied 3rd line trenches. 1 and 2 went in front of Drake lines - laid wire.

Sat. May 8th: Went back to more safe dug-outs and made same comfy. Great bombardment today. As consequence occupied 5th trenches as reserve. Stanier J. posted.

Sun. May 9th: McClelland shot in foot. In same trench. Sniper hunting all day. Weeks shot at evening.

Again and again the infantry were sent forward on the French flank, with drums beating and bugles blowing as in Napoleonic times. The New Zealanders on the left, though heavily laden with packs, shovels, picks and entrenching tools, and exposed to intense fire, advanced to within half a mile of Krithia village.

But in the failing light of the third day, the whole line, exhausted and reduced, had barely life enough to dig trenches for the night. In the centre the line had advanced 600 yards, on the flanks just 300 or 400, and the Turkish counterattack failed to recover any ground.

'We are on our last legs', wrote Sir Ian Hamilton. 'The beautiful battalions of the 25th April are wasted skeletons now; shadows of what they had been'.

The 29th Division, in continuous action for over two weeks, was brought back to the beaches for a rest - such as was possible with the beaches still under shell fire. The nights of the 11th and 12th it rained heavily and the men - caked with mud, haggard from lack of sleep, as pale as the dead, some slightly wounded, their clothes bloodstained, eyes bloodshot - just sank down into mud or pools of water, indifferent to everything except sleep.

Mon. May 10th: Spent the day improving our home, at 16 gh. 4. Left at 7pm for French at 16 ga. 4. Went up nullah to make supporting trench at 176. Was back at 3am. Sent Sharman to base with poisoned hand. Williams shot by sentry. Tired. Quiet day.

Tues. May 11: Resting all day. All very bored. Artillery came forward. Quiet again today. Men very tired. Squads 1. 8. 2. 6. 3. 7. 5. 4. 9.

Meanwhile, the folks at home had received nothing from Sydney since Port Said and with the newspapers full of the campaign, they were becoming increasingly impatient. After a page of mild complaining, Dorothy brings Sydney up to date:

Fillwood, Bishopsworth, May 5, 1915

... Uncle Arthur [Wyatt] intended driving down to Claverham [Home Farm, home of his brother, John Wyatt and family] and asked Mother to go with him, but as it was a wet morning, he jibbed, saying that he didn't see the fun of getting his trap dirty, when there are any amount of fine days coming! Mother had decided not to go anyhow, as she had another job on - that of papering her bedroom! It looks quite nice now it's done, though we weren't v. struck on the paper before it was put up.

Mrs Holbrook has been up today and we have spring-cleaned my bedroom and nearly finished Mother's. Dad and Son have been busy too, putting up the rails between 'Summerleaze' and 'Brierleaze', and a gate in the middle of them. We are expecting our usual Whit Monday party this year. (Do you remember the last one?). This time it happens to come on Empire Day and there is to be a big military demonstration in the city; a procession of all the military bodies in the district, with bands, from Queen Square to Durdham Downs, where there will be four platforms erected and big men will speak for the purpose of recruiting. Rather stirring I should think.

I heard from Alfred two days ago and to judge from his letter, nobody would think there was much the matter with him. He said there was great fun in the ward last Saturday when the doctor came in a caught him in the middle of reciting 'The Queen of the May' to two sisters and the rest of the patients, with a paper garland round his neck! The doctor almost thought that at last he had discovered Alfred's complaint!!!!! Also he had been singing to the ward and the matron is so much struck by his voice that she has given him 'Uncle Tom's Cabin' to keep him quiet! In spite of all his nonsense, he is still kept in bed and under observation; ailment not known! Laziness, I should say! He is allowed to eat anything now and says he feeds like half a dozen wolves and feels A1!!! So much for him!

Don't be surprised to hear that I've been seeing round the University, as Lieut McBain said he will at any time be delighted to show me the chemical part, while Mr James and Mr Cope-Proctor will be very pleased to take me round the rifle range etc.! My word! I wonder what they would have said if I'd named the day! They were exceedingly nice when here and not a bit swanky!

The new University building [Sir George Oatley's Wills' Memorial Building] on the Blind Asylum site is to be a beauty - magnificent architecture, after the style of Redcliffe Church, so Lieut McBain says. Wasn't it funny, we didn't hear a single shot the other night, but were all awakened by the 'come to coffee' whistle. They were very good boys, as Dad says, they didn't do ½d-worth of damage!!

Last Sunday we went to St John's and saw the vicar to speak to [The Revd John Baghot de la Bere]. He said he would have come up last Saturday, but did not feel well enough when he got half way. He was vaccinated last week [in preparation for padre duties with forces in France] and caught a chill after, but he hopes to come up soon.

Mr Langridge played the organ at Bedminster on Sunday; he plays simply beautifully. I think quite as well as Mr Hale. Our organ has been doctored, changed or something, and Mother says it's a great improvement.

Our Mr Owen is much improved too, but Harold Franklin wishes he were back at Bishopsworth again, as he doesn't like his new place at all!

Well, if this arrives with a big mail for you, you'll bless it and wish me further! So I'll shut up!

Tons of love and good wishes to you and all, from your loving sister, Dor.

Write as often as possible, if only just a postcard. I'm putting a card in with this, in case you're short.

On May 9th Win also wrote, thanking Sydney for his letter written before disembarking:

What lovely scenery you describe. It must be a real treat to you to be seeing the world as you are, of course, apart from the awfulness of things. We hear such terrible things happening, but try to think it is more than half untrue. Still hundreds of transports daily from Avonmouth. It's wonderful where they come from.

By the way, who is the 'little girl' voted the best whose photo is in your room? I can think of Nell Withers only, but you have never had much to say on that point. If you let me know, I will endeavour to forward your message.

Win was, at this stage, the helpless, rather bored, pregnant wife, sitting at home waiting for her Willie.

I have been alone all day - and only one person came to see me, and that was for ¼ of an hour only. Willie tells me that the Germans have sunk the 'Lusitania' off the Irish coast today. No details yet.

Sonnie came over last night, but only stayed a very short time, as he was so tired and hot. It has been very oppressive the last day or two and I think we shall have a heavy thunderstorm tonight.

I must write a note to Mother and enclose your letter tonight. Am so glad you are well and having such a good time, and hope it will continue. With fondest love and all good wishes, Will and Win.

An appreciable gap was widening between the world of Sgt Sydney Hall on the Dardanelles battle front and that of his family back home. He, at least, must have been more capable of entering into their world then they into his.

Mrs Hall's letter two days later is little more than a recitation of ailments: 'Gladys' slight neuralgia' and 'Maggie Hall's floating kidney'; 'Stanley Carpenter's meningitis' and 'Willie's father's stroke'; 'Aunt Sarah's condition no better', and of course, the everlastingly boring Alfred Pearce.

Needless to say, Mrs Hall trotted round in her trap to see all these malingering friends and neighbours and so missed the event of the week. Coming home from the floating kidney:

Just saw Win, by the way - should have stayed longer but Rev. Bannister and his wife had promised, or asked, if they may come over, so I felt I must hurry home and got here just as they with 3 children had finished tea! Dor is not keen on improving our acquaintance!

Talking of visiting clergymen, welcome or otherwise, Dorothy's next letter is a classic:

12 May

A few days ago, Mother wrote to you and said I would give you particulars of the visit of Mr de la Bere and Mr Champain [The former, it should be noted, was of a somewhat flirtatious disposition and, by all accounts, was rather sweet on Dorothy Hall].

So I'll make a start, though I can't possibly recount all the amusement. I was just starting to get the tea and Mother was putting herself smart on Thursday last, when the bell rang and before I got into the parlour, a tremendous pummelling of fists on the front door gave me an idea who was there, and I was not mistaken, though I certainly did not expect the vicar of Redcliffe with him! They had walked over Dundry from Flax Bourton, making, from the top of the hill, a beeline for Fillwood, over the hedges and ditches, wheat fields and what not! Needless to say, they were tired.

When tea was ready, they went upstairs to wash their hands and while there, Mrs and the two Misses Ford [wife and sisters of the vicar of Bishopsworth] arrived and just got into the parlour when Mr de la Bere came down the stairs (sliding too) in his shirt sleeves, putting on his coat on the way, and followed by Mr C.! It is difficult to decide who was the most surprised of the whole lot! After just speaking to the ladies, Mr de la Bere walked out into the sitting room where I was putting extra cups etc. and nearly made me <u>burst</u>*, by holding up his hands in dismay and saying in an awe-struck voice, 'Have you got enough?'*

He said he should begin at once unless I was <u>sure</u> *there was enough to go round! But the best bit was to follow. Mr Champain asked, 'Who are they, Baghot?' and received the reply, 'Two of them are Ford's sisters and the other - the* <u>pretty</u> *one - is Ford's wife'!*

Revd Baghot de la Bere

The face he made was enough to turn milk sour and all the time the parlour door was open and I dared not smile out loud as 'the pretty one' was too near! Oh, isn't he an <u>awful</u> *man?*

All through tea time he behaved disgracefully and I'm sure I don't know what Mr Ford had to hear that night. We couldn't help feeling a bit glad that they happened to meet here, but the two clergymen were anything but pleased! Mr de la Bere says he will come up some time during the summer for a game of tennis; hope Miss Mallard won't be jealous if he does!

Antony has marked out the court for the first time today, but the grass has not been cut yet; though we are hoping for a game soon. I wish I could have the pleasure of giving you a whacking as, of course, I should do if we could 'antagonise'! I went into town yesterday to buy a racquet, as I thought it would be better than playing with either of ours, which (with the exception of Antony's) consist of frames with remnants of strings hanging therefrom! I gave the large amount of 6/9d for my new one, so expect results!

Antony has gone to the theatre this evening to see 'Trial by Jury' and 'HMS Pinafore'. He asked Clifford to go with him, but he refused - too late at night, I expect! [Cousin Clifford Adams].

Dick Withers came up on Monday evening. He seems to be getting quite settled in his new home and business, but is without a housekeeper (Lucy having returned home) and is at the tender mercy of a daily woman! Shouldn't think it will answer very well!

Dorothy seems to have had a more realistic grasp of the war than other members of the family, and this letter ends on a grim note:

We have read in the papers the account of your landing on the Gallipoli peninsula - most stirring reading; and we only hope a large percentage will return to tell about it, and what comes after. History is being manufactured at an alarming rate nowadays! At last we hear that the mob is 'getting its back up'. and since the sinking of the 'Lusitania', Germans, their shops and goods, are having a warm time, especially in London and Liverpool! We haven't heard that Mr 'Wisserwasser' has had to run for his life yet, but it seems that the lion is just beginning to resent having his face trodden on! Time too!!

PS. [added the next morning]. In today's paper we read that Lance Corporal Harold Pearce [Alfred's brother] was killed at the front last Sunday night. He volunteered to take a party of men to put planks over wire entanglements in the German lines, and to cut the wire if possible. They went between 200 and 300 yards and were within 15 yards of the wire when a searchlight was turned on them, an order was passed down the German lines and firing commenced. Harold was the only one hit, though the others had bullets through their clothes, and he was carried back unconscious and died shortly after. We are thankful to hear that he could not have suffered; he certainly died a gallant death and his family may well be proud of him! I do feel sorry for them.

Best love, Dor.

Dorothy cut out the newspaper report and put it in her photograph album under a picture of Harold. The four photos sent by Sapper Ruddock of Sydney and company in Lemnos in early April had arrived in Fillwood and were causing some excitement. Dorothy rushed around showing them to people. Mrs Hall, 16th May:

Dor showed them to the vicar, his sisters and Miss Gardiner [Fanny and Emily Gardiner and their niece, Jessie, of Chestnut Court] on Thursday; Misses Witt (3) came to tea and Mr Rogers came in after. They also all saw them and were much interested. Mr Rogers is altered - not so fat as he used to be and still has to be careful, no cricket or games, so the Dr. says, but he intends to try cricket soon, unless he thinks better of it!

I had a letter from Uncle Joseph the other day, especially enquiring about you. He says they have done 'magnificently' at the Dardanelles. Have you seen Capt. Page since you landed? I expect not. Another worry for the poor man - a Zeppelin visited Southend, dropping bombs which caused fires in Westcliff and other places, very near 'White Heather', but Jean and Mary are alright. Jean is getting stronger and the babies are splendid, so they say.

And lots more about Maggie's floating kidney and Alfred Pearce's 'cocked hat', and:

... we are expecting Willie over for a walk with his father, who is, I am sorry to say, putting on the childish old man fast. They came over last Sunday and he went back tired and slept well - a wonder for him lately, I believe. The Dr. fears a stroke for him and has told Willie, so they feel anxious.

It is Willie's birthday today - 28 - so I hope he'll come to have some scalded cream.

Mr Moon enquired for you this morning - he is watching news from the Dardanelles closely. They heard from Maurice on Tuesday, he is well but glad to get a parcel of grub - good things every week. I am wondering if you get enough, if not, I'm afraid cakes would be rather stale if we sent them, but I hope you are better supplied. I shall have another lot of chocolate and coconut ice sent this week, I hope, though we do not know if you ever received the other.

It's horribly wet and cold today - at least it changes so often. This morning the air was very soft, now tonight it's quite cold and we need a cheery fire. Dad is quite bonny again, I'm glad to say, and prospects at present are good - fruit trees in magnificent bloom, so we may hope for an abundant harvest and thankful shall we be, for the good of ourselves and our country, it seems a harbinger of victory! I shall get Alfred [Pitman] to post this presently. Hoping you are well, love and best wishes to you and Good Luck to R.N.D.D.E. and God Bless You,

Your affectionate Mother.

Alfred Pearce, we are delighted to hear, had at last been discharged from hospital. Clara (26th), Dorothy (20th) and Win (21st) all report on his ailments, which seem to have ranged from bronchitis, influenza and over-tiredness, to suspected consumption. He was released early it seems because of the death of his brother, and 'all his family were very down in the dumps when he arrived, so he played the giddy goat to wake them up ...' and lost no time in coming to Fillwood to dance attendance on Dorothy. He stayed a few days, went to visit the shocking Revd Baghot de la Bere, vicar of Bedminster in the pouring rain, and his younger brother interrupted Dorothy's next letter to Sydney (20th May):

I had just started to write when I had to fill my pen, which I'd just done when Eddie P. arrived, bringing back an umbrella and a pair of trousers, or rather waterproof legs which we had lent Alfred last Monday.

Alfred asked Baghot de la Bere to come up to Fillwood for tennis. He <u>didn't</u> come for tennis, but he <u>did</u> come for tea and talk.

No doubt fearing his rival was overtaking him in Dorothy's affections, the vicar was probably relieved to hear that Alfred was to start his studies again the next day. And we hear again about the newlyweds setting off for India to convert the heathen.

Mother heard from Mrs Theodore Page (née Miss Chapman) today, to say she and her hubby hope to come here for a little holiday before they start for India. I must go to bed now, so please forgive this rotten letter and hope for better next time. Talking and writing letters do not do well together. [Amy Pavey - an old family friend was visiting].

From Win:

May 21 1915

My Dear Syd,

How are you getting on all this long time? Having a lively time I should say by the papers, if nothing else. Well, I hope you have come through safely up to now and will continue to do so. Of course, we have not expected to hear from you, as you seem to have had nothing but continued fighting since you last wrote on April 23rd ...

I know I wouldn't like it if Willie were over in France, but I know he would go like a shot if it were not for me. Now they are thinking of bringing conscription. I suppose he will have to go at some time, and then hope I shan't worry too much.

I have not seen mother since last Friday, but Antony and Dad were in yesterday - market day. Dad bought a lovely rose tree and, of course, I thought, 'Oh, a present for me', but no such luck, he carried it on to Fillwood. It wasn't fair, was it?

I expect Willie will go to Fillwood either tomorrow, Sunday or Monday (Bank Holiday), but I shan't be able to manage the journey just yet. Well, old chap, goodbye for this time, and good luck to 'ee. With fondest and best love from both. I remain your loving sister, Win.

Though his family were not to know for weeks yet, Sydney's pocket book tells us the 'lively time' he was having:

Wed. May 12: Spitlocking road all day. Under orders to continue trench work last night, but too many infantry were going up the nullah, so we stayed and sentry neglected to wake us up at midnight. Wet night and wet today. Not nice.

The centre of the Gallipoli plateau slopes gently inwards like a saucer, with the highest land along the clifftops. As the front line was pushed across it, protection was needed from the shells bursting from the Kum Kale battery across the straits, and the Turkish lines to the north. The Engineers in the RND were responsible for constructing roads, and later a rail track to bring up the heavy guns. As these approached the centre of the declivity, deep trenches - 10 feet wide and 8 feet deep - were run first horizontally across the plateau and then longitudinally northwards. In most places it was possible to make use of the nullahs or dried up beds of small streams which drained from the north and then east into Morto Bay.

All hands were at work on these massive operations in the lulls between fighting. Sydney's company was principally engaged in engineering works and, when occasion required, digging new trenches, and during the major offensive, actually manning the 2nd and 3rd lines.

Thurs. 13th: Had a working party on the road today. Carrying on. Got 4 letters from home [he doesn't say which, but presumably those written between 29th April and 5th May]. Great Luck. Turks use 6" shells on the base.

The 'base' he referred to was probably the enormous bunker which had been excavated out of a convenient hillock in the middle of the hollow. The walls inside were 20-25 feet deep in places and still today it remains a very impressive, though much overgrown, dugout.

Friday 14: Continuing road. Getting some sunburnt.

Sat. 15: Same game. Met Gough today. His coy is relieving ours. Continued road back to beach this afternoon [W Beach evidently].

Sun. May 16: Still on road, past marine HQ - now getting well towards W Beach.

Mon. 17th: Shifted camp to near French lines again. Had a day's rest. Digging funk holes. [French lines were on the east side of peninsula].

Tues. 18th: On road again: culvert covered and odd bits finished. Some shelling. Advance tonight. Had letter from Dor.

Wed. 19th: A rest day - unessayed. Lieut Tollust pipped [killed].

Thurs. 20th: More rest. Going into front line again tonight. Lieut Oakden shot. Went at 8pm with section to communication trench - deepening and widening. Came back safe at 4.30am. Very tired. Many sick men, including me a little.

Friday 21st: Rest all day; sleeping and night's rest too. Great luck.

Sat. 22nd: Rest day. Odd jobs round camp. Turned out at night on communication trench between brown ho. and ruin. Also made screen round field dressing station. Returned 4.45am.

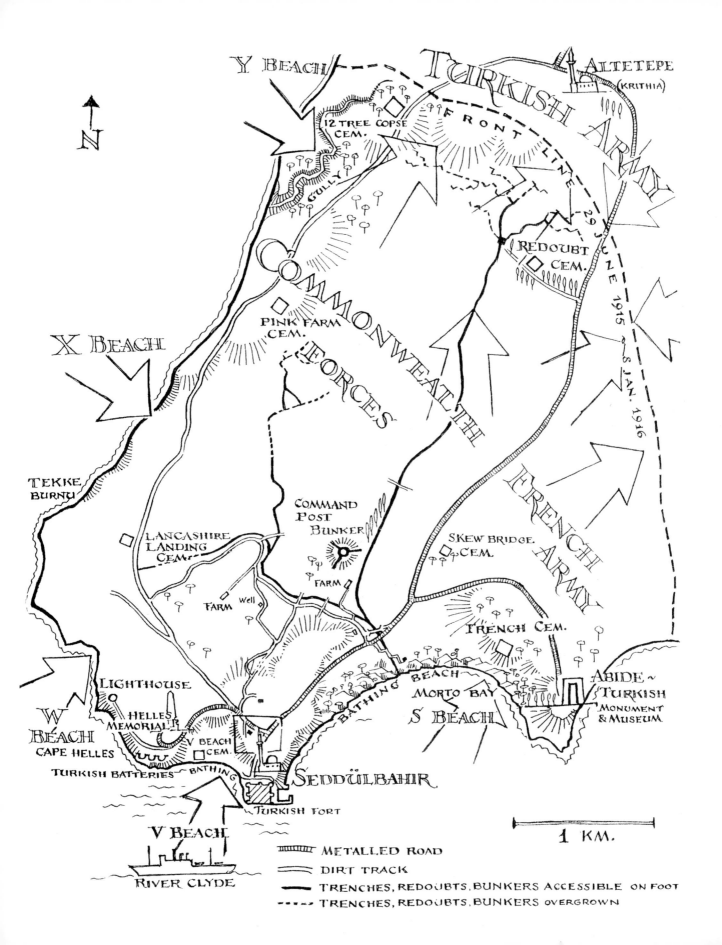

On that day, before night duties presumably, Sydney took four leaves out of his pocket book and scribbled a letter to his father in pencil:

Dear Dad,

Seeing that I have some leisure now, and that you home folks are probably anxious for any news, I am down on the job. I often feel I ought to write more when I have the chance, but it isn't much I'm allowed to tell, and not much more that I would if I could. However, you'll have seen the newspapers, and will probably know as much about the campaign as we, and when you get this, much more than we do at present. Suffice it to say that our estimate of the difficulties changed in the same way as did those of the people at home, but as for the achievements, there again you have the latest news.

That's somewhat cryptic, and very unprofitable, so let's drop it. For personal news there isn't much, but I'm quite well and not uncomfortable, though for 3 weeks my lodging has been on the cold ground with not much under me and less on top. I've been able to keep fairly clean at intervals, and my underclothes have had a wash or two, so although if you met me out you'd wonder what new piebald suitings were being worn, inwardly I'd defy the insect tribe and sorenesses (you may remember that I was never bitten by a flea yet). The food we get is excellent, though I find it an awful nuisance to get it prepared and distributed to my men, and the water supply is plentiful and good, although it's affected some men's internal economy, their interiors being more delicate than stable.

We have had spells of hard work in a slightly enervating climate and at times have been very tired, but just lately have not been so hard-pressed, so our dugout homes are an important asset nowadays, and pay for labour spent on them. Mine is a storeyed affair; the ground I walk on, and it collects rain water; No. 2 I sleep on; No. 3 sit on; No. 4 serves as a table and general store, so I've got quite an establishment.

When we are out at work we are never safe; though it's seldom any fire is directed at us purposely as we are insignificant, or appear so. Usually it's only a bore being under fire, one may or may not get pipped, according as providence decrees, so one has to be prepared, and I personally feel indifferent but for the sakes of you people at home, but I'm being as cheerful as I care to be.

I have lots of letters from home and am always glad to get them, <u>not</u> as Dorothy hinted some time back. Dor's last tells of sweets consigned, happy news; hope they'll come soon. I like to hear about people at home, the various groups I was mixed with, but I haven't energy or interest enough to write to representative members. I only write home, so I hope you'll collect little ----? when you can, as indeed you have done.

One magpie has just passed, so I'll slide into a nature talk ... [and then follows the passage about the countryside, already quoted].

I haven't written to Win for quite a time, please excuse me. I think of her nevertheless. I hope you've all had a good time on Son's tennis court. He must have worked hard on it; wouldn't I just like a foursome now, with some people I could tell you of. In lieu of cricket, whenever I've been out and about and feeling so, I take a stone and bowl a tree out. Only wish the Kaiser, Sultan or other bad cricketers were there to get lbw. Some spite.

Oh, tell Dor I'm sorry to hear about poor old A.G.P., and trust he'll be alright yet for his cocked hat. Also give my congrats to Belle Stevens, some surprise, by Jove. Thought she had collared that ass of a student, Purdue. Have had a letter from Ron and he wants me to bring him back a Sphinx or some souvenirs. I suppose souvenirs will be of value, but it's not for me to loot the 'Sphinkses' or lug pyramids about, so I'll part my raiment when I get home, so promise him a holy relic - one puttee.

Well, in addition to boring the censor, I fear I shall bore you - so I'll stop this in the usual way, with best love to all, Your slip-shod son, Syd.

As May gave way to June, English villages - and Bishopsworth was no exception - made themselves ready for the summer. Tennis courts were rolled and squared, Edwin Wyatt called a meeting of the cricket club, there was talk of summer frocks and hay-making and, as usual, weddings were more than plentiful.

Bishopsworth Cricket Club, probably a little earlier than 1915. In the back row, Arthur Wyatt is second from the left, and Edwin Light Wyatt second from the right

In Gallipoli, the coming of the summer made little difference, except for the flies. Always a nuisance, they became a menace and finally a plague. They came fresh from the tins of putrefying food tossed into no-man's-land; from blackening bodies in the scrub or on the wire and from the excrement in the Turkish trenches. They got into the eyes, nostrils, lips; descended on every morsel of food and pursued it into the mouths and down the throats of the toiling troops as they ate. There were outbreaks of dysentery and boredom and frustration, for the campaign which had been intended to break the deadlock on the Western Front became yet another stalemate.

Sir Ian Hamilton to his wife, 20th May 1915:

I am beset with nightmares dreadful enough to turn the head of 'un homme serieux', but that you know I am not, never was and never will be as long as a spark of life exists within my poor carcass. I am so interested and pleased about what you are doing for our masses of wounded - casualties are mounting up to heights absolutely terrific, for the whole Turkish army is coming at us in relays and we have to keep wiping out fresh troops from Constantinople, Syria, Adrianople, with our poor old remnants who have been at it now for a month.

My dear Syd, [wrote his mother on Whit Monday, 24th May]

We have the usual Bank Holiday crews. Mr Thomas has just been in to square up. The weather is simply gorgeous, not sun, but high wind to temper the heat, but not too rough for Will, Dor and Antony to be having a game of tennis. Poor old Win was afraid to venture her precious self, and so is either having a visitor for company or gone out to tea at Elm Bank. I am going in tomorrow for the day - she is embarking on the luxuries of a servant! Hope she'll be a success. Just now they are very expensive luxuries - higher wages as well as the grub to feed them with! Beef gone up 2d. a lb. this last week, a fortune for those who have a few fat cattle - bankruptcy for the poor housekeeper.

Interrupted - May 26th.

Hooray! A letter from you dated May 1st!!! So thankful to get it, to hear you were well and happy. But what lots has happened since then. A very full account of the doings at the Dar in this morning's paper, but even with such full accounts, how little can we realise all that is happening.

I went to Win's yesterday and Will came over here for tennis ... and they had a good time, I think. Win was feeling well and we spent the afternoon in the back garden with our fancy work and a bit of gardening in between, and we had quite a happy time on the quiet. Dad has put up a natural wood arch in the garden, just by the moss-rose. Son is starting a bit of photography with Horton's camera, so must get him to send a snap of it to you. Mab and Clifford [Mabel Adams, her widowed cousin, and her small son] came to tea yesterday, after going to Mr George Adams' funeral at Whitchurch; they didn't stay long.

Poor old Stanley [Carpenter] is still isolated at Millbank Military Hospital; they say his throat is still infectious. I am not going to write any more now - I must leave some news for Dor tomorrow. Heaps of love dear boy from your loving mother.

But Win got in first:

Once more 'tis Friday evening, the No. 44 Belluton Road letter-writing evening, so here goes for a letter to you, but can't guarantee much news 'cause there ain't much.

Dor came in yesterday on her way to town where she was going to buy a new hat. Fearful swank, I can tell you. She also came back this way to show it off. I must say she looks quite smart as usual in it ...

Here's Dor's account:

On Thursday I went to Win's and into town to buy myself a new hat - awful 'nutty', black with a large pink rose and foliage, to wear with my evening dress which is to be altered for day wear!!!

Back to Win:

Dad came in to tea on his way back from market. He is looking ever so much better than I've ever seen him. I think he's much brighter too and does not complain quite so much. I have not been near the fields for some time now, but Will tells me the crops look very good and especially Homemead. Of course, that is always good, isn't it? Mr de la Bere is going to help haymaking this year (so he says) so it will be done much earlier than usual, as you may guess. By the way, that gentleman seems to be nearly living at Fillwood lately. I'm thinking somebody ought to enquire into things ...

Dorothy's version:

On Wednesday, Mother and Dad intended starting after an early tea for Castle Farm and Highridge [homes of Ben's sister, Hester Elizabeth Froud, and Clara's sister, Sarah Britton and her family], but when we were halfway through tea, that dear Vicar of Bedminster arrived on the scene - greatly shocked to find he was late. He had taken one of the 'Cowley Fathers' to S. Agnes' Home and walked across the fields, and I was quite shocked (I don't think) when he told me that the Misses Gardiner had invited him to tennis that afternoon, but having made up his mind to come here, he told them he was too busy! Isn't he an old hypocrite?

After tea he and I played a single in which I was hopelessly whacked 6-3!! He asked for and obtained permission to bring the Sunday School children up here for their treat this year, as Weston excursions are off; so I suppose they will come the end of next month if the hay-making in Homemead is finished by then. After the gent had gone, Mother and Dad did their tour [no question of leaving Dor alone with him] - very pleased to be able to tell the folks that at last we had heard from you!

Dorothy must have been conscious that tongues were wagging and attempted to direct the interest to Sydney's 'young lady', Lucy Withers, taunting him with the news that she had got herself engaged to 'Farmer Boulton, the bailiff at Lower Court', then adding: *So that you should not despair unnecessarily, perhaps I had better tell you that the bride-to-be is not your Lucy, but her esteemed mother! Wonders will never cease!!!*

Actually Sydney had many young lady admirers, but no-one special - so it was all a bit of sisterly leg-pulling. We hear nothing about the girl he really admired, Una Brookhouse Richards, so he must have kept quiet about her.

Back to Win:

Willie is doing a little more carpentering to improve the 'appy 'ome. He's always working either at gardening, painting or summat else, except when he's in bed. Enough said.

I believe they have been making good use of the tennis court at home the last week and have had some good games. Dor said yesterday that the court is cracking through for want of rain, but I don't think they mind much as long as the weather keeps as fine as it has been lately ...

Mother had your letter of May 1st yesterday, so was very excited. You seem to be having a good time up to then, but there is a tough lot to do before you finish, I think.

Mrs Evans [her mother-in-law] had a P.C. from Jack this morning [Will's younger brother was at the Front]. He is still all right. Arthur Russell saved again by about 2 minutes, having just left the trench when it was blown to atoms. Young Sweet of Dundry killed [Upton Farm]. Have not heard anything of Maurice Moon, but Grace and Sidney seem to be getting on alright. They stayed at Ma Moon's for Whitsuntide.

Will shut up now. With fondest and best from us both, Will and Win.

Over to Dor again:

... talking about weddings, there was a very swank one over at Bishopsworth last week, when the lady from the King's Head, Miss Butcher, married a baker named Willie Needham! White satin gown, two bridesmaids, three carriages and pairs and a private motor car - concluded by a big bust-up at West Street Chapel - free drinks at the King's Head and an injured policeman!!!! Sad to say I did not receive an invitation and only heard of the free drinks after they were all gone!

Amy Pavey stayed again. She was a great chatterbox, which can be gauged from the number of exclamation marks Dorothy used after almost every reference to her:

Yesterday Amy and I cycled to Whitchurch Green and back to church in the evening. All well there except that Mr J. Vowles is still itching! [Ben Hall's brother-in-law]. They are expecting that Bert will have to join something shortly; his name is down, to be called if wanted, I suppose.

We had a long letter from Jean this morning, containing the news that you returned to the 'Ayrshire' after your baptism of fire. Evidently she was your H.Q. for some time. Poor old Jean has had her share of worry lately. Perhaps you have heard that Southend has been visited a second time by Zeppelins and she writes that this time was heaps worse than the first, when there were several fires within a stone's throw of White Heather; for they say two Zeps go over and one of them stopped directly over their house and they just waited for the bomb to fall. Happily, however, they didn't get one. She had a letter from the Captain on Tuesday - the first for a month - as ours from you!

The day that this letter was written, Sydney was wounded - not seriously - but enough to put him out of action for several days. After a lull in the middle of May, events began working up to a climax and the laconic entries in the pocket book give an indication of the rising temperature.

<u>Sun. 23 Whit Sunday</u>: Roe and Mawson promoted to Lieutenant. Holy Communion service this morning. Queerest I ever knew. Section 1 told off this evening for 3 days front line work, and the men distributed in trenches on jobs. Some night! Several working parties.

<u>Mon. 24</u>: 2 hours sleep. Working parties all day - draining. Marked out trenches for advance tonight for whole R.N.D. brigade in trenches. Lancashire on our flank, later went up and met Gough. Back 12.45am in trenches. Roberts shot in leg. Ar hyd y nos. [All through the night].

<u>Tues. 25</u>: Getting even in trenches all day. Two thunderstorms put all wrong again. Also brigades changed in firing line. Had working parties till 2.30am; then worked pump all rest of night.

<u>Wed. 26</u>: Some mess still, but sun dries things quickly. Men dead tired. I slept while writing report. Let sun do his work. Relieved at about 6pm. Back in some state at rest camp.

At this point there is a sketch plan of some trenches, presumably those that his section had been endeavouring to drain of rain water that collected in the central, concave floor of the Gallipoli plateau. Lack of space in the pocket book prevented further entries, so Sydney turned to the end and from then on the entries work backwards.

THE ZEPPELIN RAID OF MAY 10: DAMAGE AT SOUTHEND AND LEIGH.

PHOTOGRAPHS NOS. 1 AND 2 BY C.N.; 3, GRAPHIC PHOTO UNION; 4, PHOTOPRESS; 5 AND 7, L.N.A.; 6, TOPICAL.

A WRECKED BEDROOM IN THE CROMWELL BOARDING-HOUSE, LONDON ROAD, SOUTHEND.

ANOTHER VIEW OF THE WRECKED BEDROOM IN THE CROMWELL BOARDING-HOUSE, LONDON ROAD.

A COMPLETELY GUTTED HOUSE IN BAXTER AVENUE. SOUTHEND.

THE BADLY DAMAGED CROMWELL BOARDING-HOUSE IN LONDON ROAD, SOUTHEND.

A STREET SCENE SHOWING DAMAGED HOUSES IN WEST STREET, SOUTHEND.

THE BED THROUGH WHICH A BOMB PASSED, IN CRANLEIGH DRIVE, LEIGH-ON-SEA.

A VERY BADLY DAMAGED HOUSE IN SOUTH STREET. SOUTHEND.

'The Illustrated London News', May 15, 1915

<u>Thurs. May 27</u>: What a sleep last night! Rest day and out for advance of RND tonight. Rather a hot job. May and Robson killed. Roe injured. Got out 200 yards. Back 1.30.

<u>Friday 28th</u>: Rest day. Bathing parade in afternoon (Morto Bay). Had mail and shell at tea time. Dressed at 3rd F.A. [Field Ambulance] where stayed the night.

He began a letter to his mother before he was injured:

May 28th

Dear Mother,

Dor's idea of sending this paper was great. I must use it for usual purpose of telling you that I am well. I'm just recovering from fatigue, for we've had 7½ hours almost continuous duty of first line work, a great test of endurance. I hope this somewhat trying work is done for some time, for we've had some men on the verge of collapse. You will be pleased to hear that this unit has gained a name, and even been mentioned in dispatches - for steadiness, and I can assure you that the chaps have merited it.

Well, my last mail was a great one. I had letters from Dor, Win and Son, and of course, the newspaper. I don't know if you noticed but it was announced that on Apr. 30th, the night of the scrap [night operation at Fillwood] Dr McBain became a father. The attack must have been a farce, I wish I'd been there to show 'em. I was so pleased to get the account, however.

Win's letters, otherwise most proper and instructive, were made humorous by the unsuccessful attempt to guess the name of this girl I mentioned. If I remember rightly, I was in a sentimental mood that morning and thought I had 'found the Queen' in my collection, but these postcard tricks don't always work alike, so I keep my money, and tongue, and Naval Reserve.

It's all very amusing. I got Dor's sweets, but they did not arrive in such good condition as they left, although they're still very nice. I am afraid that my motions must remain mysterious, for when I say we're moving tomorrow it means D.V. and after D. now V. That is one of the trials of war. Am so glad to hear that AGP is not so seriously ill, I hope he's quite well by now. Son's letter was great, I wish he'd write oftener, however much 'lies and rot' he puts in. I'm interested in the movements of Dick and Edie, good luck to 'em. Oh, I met Gough again, under quite romantic circs, gosh, shan't we have a jaw-pie if and when we get out!

I'm off now to take the chaps for a swim, so must shut off, only waiting to give my fond love and kind remembrances to all of 'ours'. I often have a good think about them, a sort of, 'Oh, to be there' feeling, but work first. Your loving son, Syd.

29th. When I came back from the bathing parade, I sat down in my parlour and prepared to take a little tea. Then two interesting things arrived. One was some letters, one of Dor's, one of yours, and a paper. The other was a high explosive shell which fell on my parapet and heaved a great stone at me, which made some bruises. I only had one splinter taken out and as I'm not inconvenienced, I can carry on, my section being due for a couple of days rest. The shell, a 4" one, didn't seriously hurt anyone, though one chap was struck 50 yards away. The Turkish artillery is rotten. After the bump, I sat down and laughed at it.

With regard to your letter, I'm sorry to hear news of Maggie, but hope she's better now. Also Dor's news of Harold Pearce. Dor's account of Mr de la Bere and co. was very humorous; to put it coldly, I bet he's a scream. I wish Dor would treat herself to a decent racquet (also Son) at my expense, if I have any funds available. If not, try and get some out with the enclosed bit of black paper, or forge my signature on one of these forms. Best and fondest, Syd. Yes, that's me in the Lemnos picture. Gosh, didn't I work that day!

On the 30th, little Ida Withers, who had been at Avonmouth on that bleak March morning to see Sydney off, wrote in a childish hand:

Glenmere, Clapton

Dear Syd,

Being Sunday evening and not going to church, I thought to write you a few lines to let you know we are still in the land of the living. Only Britton and mother are gone to church. Britton's latest is shearing sheep. We hear now that Britton and Stanley Lever have taken over 80 to shear, they start tomorrow, so I expect he will be up by time in the morning. We had two shearers here four days last week, so ours are finished.

About 6 weeks ago there was a 'Scouts Concert' given in aid of the Sailors and Soldiers held in Clapton School. The Misses Morgan were there and bright sparks they are too. Dad hopes to be able to start haymaking in about 3 weeks' time. We are very well off for men at the present ...

We have two nice cart colts this year. Ever so many of the shows are put off this year. Mr Snook is a little better but he seems in bed very often still.

The North Somersets have been in hard fighting again and have been badly cut up. George is alright. We heard from Ernest Withers the other day; he has joined the North Somersets.

Your little godchild [her sister, Ruth] seems to grow a little now. She talks very plainly and is on with some of her fun now. I cannot think of any more to say, and it looks as though some of the children are nearly ready for bed, so goodbye.

Hoping you are still alive and kicking. As it leaves us fairly well. With love (only cousinly, of course!), From Ida

P.S. Ruth sends two kisses to God-pa, but as I cannot spare as many as that, I suppose I must send a half one. Hope you won't break down under this awful load.

Her mother added:

Fido has just glanced through this. We often think of you and wish you a safe return. Antony cycled down with Clifford one Sunday lately. I saw Win a week ago. All's well. Yours, F.

On the same day, from his mother:

Success to all the RNDDE.

My dear Syd,

Dad and I have just returned from a walk round the farm where things are in a fairly forward condition. Signs of plenty of work in the course of a week or two. How I wish you were here to help. We were so glad to get your letter dated May 1st. What a time it was coming - 25 days. I wonder if we shall have to wait so long again.

I had a letter yesterday from Jean. She also had heard from Will and wrote to tell us so. Also that they had escaped unhurt from the Zeppelin raid this week, though a Zep passed over her house twice, and stopped once, and they were waiting and expecting a bomb to fall. She said her heart was in her mouth while the danger lasted and they felt 'anyhow' all the next day. Poor little Jean, she has had a hard time the last 12 months, and Will away. What she would have done without Mary I can't think. But there, Mary was with her!

Will [Evans] has just been over. Marion Powell was at home with Winnie. Wouldn't their chins wag when left alone! They have not seen each other for some months. Marion's boy [she means her young man] is at the Dardanelles, at the Cavalry Headquarters, I believe, but I dare say Win will tell you all about him.

Tuesday June 2nd. Dor has just been to Bishopsworth for rent [the Halls owned a few cottages on the village triangle, including the Old Chapel cottages, which they rented out for 2/6d per year], and has brought back your first field post-card. So glad to receive it and the news 'I am quite well'. I fancy you have some heavy fighting, but we can only hope success will crown your efforts. I presume the 'Ayrshire' is kept near the beach for 'lodging' and rest instead of camps. I wish you could tell us! Are all your chums quite well? I hope so. Remember me to the Captain when you see him. I wrote to Jean suggesting she came here for a long stay with her babies and Mary, but I hardly think she will care to leave, even though it is on the 'East Coast' and liable to enemy raids. I shall hear in a day or two.

Sister Win wrote:

June 3rd, 1915

My dear Syd,

I saw one of those beautiful P.C.s from you yesterday dated May 11th. Dor came over in the evening and brought it to show me. She came over specially for a pattern for a dress though. Oh, these girls, how they <u>do</u> dress ...

Can you find a servant for us among the Turks etc. Willie has spent quite a nice lot of money on advertising etc. and we can't get one somehow. They are more scarce than ever now and I really doubt if we <u>shall</u> get one.

Marion Powell came here on Sunday for the first time since June 9th last year. Her intended husband is out your way; stationed mostly at Alexandria. He is sort of a clerk to headquarters, or summat grand like that. His name is Sergeant Robertson. Very dark chap. Don't know if you'll run up against him.

Poor Antony had a nice job today - shearing a rotten sheep. He said he didn't want to get too near. I should think not indeed.

My poor little hubby has caught one of his most awful colds somewhere. Can't think where; for weather has been simply perfect. He is feeling very seedy, but hope he will soon get better ...

Well, old chap, I will dry up now. With fondest love from Will and Win.

Back to Clara Hall:

Dor had a letter from Alfred this morning. He is apparently alright again; complaining of heat, but here we have had a sharp frost, cutting potatoes and beans in many gardens. Glad to say ours did not suffer. We had young potatoes last Sunday and Sunday week. Vicar was here to tea last night - he could scarcely believe it when I told him! Clifford is here tonight learning tennis! The court is fine, so they say!

I am enclosing a bit of today's paper, thought it would interest you. You have never said if you received the Easter cakes or chocolates. We want to send more if only we knew you would get it. Much love, dear boy, from us all. We are all so thankful to know you were well, and hope you still are. Your loving mother.

But all was not well with Sydney. The terse pocket book entries do not tell the whole story.

Sunday 30th May: Communion service in morning. Section making fascines.

Mon. 31 May: Section on camp duties. Been dl'd up in evening to make sops. Spent night thereon.

Tues. June 1: Came down grub hunting and copper wound got septic. Am sent back to HQ. State of Section: Effectives 15; Here 26; Killed 2; Wd 7.

Wed: Resting.

Thurs: do.

Friday 4th: do. Grand attack. French fail.

5th: Quieter.

The Anzacs hanging onto their clifftops 20 miles away were incapable of making any advance, so it was up to the allies at the other end of the peninsula to make another push to reach them.

On Friday 4th June, Sir Ian Hamilton and the French General Gouraud ordered a major offensive along the whole Helles front. On 30th May Sir Ian to his wife:

No-one is going to help us but ourselves and all the power of Turkey is concentrating against us - still, are we downhearted? No.

The so-called Third Battle of Krithia opened with a massive bombardment of the enemy lines from both land and sea. At 11.20 the front line was ordered to fix bayonets and present them over their parapets, in order to bring the Turks into their trenches. It was a ruse which succeeded admirably, for instead of the infantry advance that was expected, the enemy trenches were subjected to another intensive pounding by artillery, although the shell fire from the ships often fell wide of the mark as they had to keep moving to avoid torpedoes.

The devastating barrage lifted at noon and from end to end of the line the men sprang from their trenches. The attack opened brilliantly. On the left flank, the Manchester Brigade and the Gurkhas cleared the Turkish positions and advanced to the foothills of Achi Baba, almost encircling Krithia village from the west. In the centre, the RND swept through first and second Turkish lines. On the right, the French captured the formidable Turkish redoubt at Kereves Dere, which had so long held them up, but at this point the advance faltered. Kereves Dere proved a death trap. The Turkish artillery blasted it with high explosives, followed by an overwhelming counterattack. The French were forced to pull back to their original positions.

The RND, now exposed on their right, were cruelly enfiladed and were forced to pull back too, leaving the Manchesters stranded. They too, after terrible losses, were extricated by sunset.

65

TWO DAYS BEFORE THE FRENCH COMMANDER WAS GRIEVOUSLY WOUNDED: GENERAL SIR IAN HAMILTON VISITING
GENERAL GOURAUD TO ANNOUNCE A SUCCESS NEAR KRITHIA.

'The Illustrated London News', June 17, 1915

Sir Ian Hamilton to his wife:

5.6.1915

I was in battle all yesterday. The troops did splendidly but these Turks are so fortified and so entrenched, and they bring up so many fresh troops, that we can only gain ground by continued ghastly sacrifices. I suppose all these conspirators and intriguers will begin to occupy themselves with poor me before long ...

Apart from a few hundred yards in the centre, the whole operation had been a costly failure. The casualties were appalling. The Hampshires lost all their officers, and only 100 men were left. The 1st Lancashire Fusiliers had 14 officers and 500 men killed or wounded. The Indian Brigade had shot its bolt - all four battalions were decimated and the survivors had to be amalgamated with other divisions.

Worst of all as far as Sydney was concerned, the RND - very largely due to their intrepid fighting spirit - suffered the most. There were 1,170 casualties, including 40 officers. Their losses were so severe that two battalions (Benbow and Collingwood) had to be disbanded.

<u>Sunday June 6th</u>: Rowdy night and morning. Skinner wounded.

From the HQ where he was still recovering from his wounds, Sydney wrote a letter to his mother that day. Though the tone is still jaunty, there are signs of weariness and frustration. It was the nearest he came to cracking up. While he had heaps to do, there had not been time to think; but put out of action, despondency set in - a realisation that the whole campaign had ground to a halt and on top of that, the fact that the RND, of which he was so proud, had been cut to pieces and he not able to do his part.

Dear Mother,

Since I wrote last a few things have happened. You remember I was slightly wounded. Well, I carried on with the Section for 2 or 3 days till one of the wounds began to fester a bit, so then I had to stop. (I've got two wounds on the right side of my back, one about ½ inch, and the other ¾ inch deep. This one is a lowdown hit! Rather!!)

So then I came down to the rest camp to give the beggars a chance and here I am now. Since here, I've had time to notice the disadvantages of the place as a convalescent home - it's not ideal. The flies are getting awful since the nights became warmer. I hope they're not so bad everywhere. If you ever feel spiteful on my account, kill a fly. Then there are 3 or 4 batteries just near and their noise and the shells that are fired back at them don't conduce to peacefulness much. Combine these with great need of caution when taking a seat, and imagine my present state of jolliness.

To stop grousing. I beg to state that I have had a letter from Dor and also one from Win since I wrote last. I note and thank them for news received. Remember me to Horton and to Mrs Th. Page. Also congratulate Alfred from me on his recovery. Is Win right when talking of probable conscription? I have seen nothing in the papers recently about it.

I should have written before, but I hadn't any note paper. But everybody seems to have run out. By great good fortune only did I meet a man this morning who gave me three of these. So please send me some stationery. (They'll probably serve it out the day before your consignment arrives).

I should also like 2 pairs of thin knee-length pants, Aertex or similar, and two pairs of socks, fairly thick; also 3 handkerchiefs.

Then, in a rare fit of nostalgia, in words that could have been penned by Rupert Brooke, himself a victim of the Dardanelles war:

Well, I'm thinking how does the garden grow and is the hay crop good and are the horses in good condition and the wheat fields blooming? And oh, has the reaper been repaired? And has the cuckoo done and the landrail begun; and does anyone wish old Siddie was there ... ? Yes, he does! Well, after these thinkings, I think that I'd better stop thinking. I met another Bristol (MV) man in the trenches the other day, named Cockey. The operations here are much too sticky for my liking; they say that Achi Baba is on wheels, and the more we advance, the more it recedes. However, we'll catch the beggar some day I hope. The usual brand of love to all. Syd

Am also in need of a watch - a 6/6d Ingersoll will do well enough.

PS. Forgot to say I am now Sgt Major. PPS. Also that wounds are healing well.

Haymaking on a Bishopsworth farm in the early twentieth century

The promotion was, no doubt, due to the appalling losses over the last 48 hours, though it must be admitted young Sydney Hall was more than capable of handling this new responsibility and would have come to it anyway, sooner or later.

His mother wrote the same day:

My dear Syd,

Amy came up to dinner with us today and, before I forget it, I must give you her message. Her love, of course, comes first, and she wishes me to say they have nearly cut up the rick of hay you made and it has turned out very well, and she is very anxious that you should know it! Also that Auntie [Amy's mother, Sarah] is better and they still live in hope that they will be able to have her home once more, with a trained nurse, but not just yet perhaps!

We all wish you were home to help with the work this year! Not that we shall have less men than usual, but Alfred came in quite unexpectedly just now and has gone to church or the Common [Highridge Farm], I wouldn't like to say which! The last time he came up he didn't go to see Aunt Ada at all, naughty boy! She came up last night and seemed very hurt about it, and as Dor wasn't here, I had to let him down lightly. Today he went there before coming here, so it's all right now. As he says, 36 hours leave is none too much to see everybody in and he is bound to go to Bishopsworth to see all the aunts and give them a kiss! I wonder he isn't bilious when he goes back after so many sweets! We are all wondering what he'll do with his sword when he has to wear one. Will he wear it over his shoulder, or let it drag the ground hanging from his belt?!!

Willie hasn't been over tonight, so I imagine his cold is still very bad. Poor fellow seemed very wretched on Friday ...

We are having young potatoes every Sunday since Whit Sunday - very good, but very small. Wanting rain badly for everything. I am afraid we shall have very few strawberries unless we get some. It has threatened several days, but that is all and blight is terrible on all the flowers - no roses except the red ones in the pantry, up to now. My tree is a sad spectacle, leaves falling off, looking scorched with blight.

We are all living in hope that we shall have a letter from you this week - we eagerly watch for the post daily. All are well, and we sincerely hope you are too. Heaps of love, dear boy, from Mother.

Dorothy, the same day:

My dear Syd,

At last it's come to Sunday for my letter to be written. We were regularly full up all last week, so I couldn't manage to squeeze in a line. Amy Pavey was here for last weekend and after she started for school on Monday morning, Mother and I set to work to spring clean the parlour. Of course, it was not by any means finished when we stopped at tea-time, though the worst part was done. After tea, Mrs White, Lucy and Floss Snook arrived on the scene, so the evening was filled with tennis and talk.

Next day we finished our fancy job and then I had to go for the rent. When I returned, Clifford was here for a game, so that evening was booked. He promises to make a good tennis player, with a bit of practice, and I think it's quite likely we shall often see him here during the season, except, of course, when harvesting prevents.

On Wednesday I went over to see Win and on Thursday we had quite a party here for tennis - one which would have suited you down to the ground. John [Britton] was the first to arrive and Katie Evans [Will's sister] came next. Then Annie Milward [from school] and Mr Ford - to tea, all of them! Afterwards May, Dorothy and Kathleen and a Miss Adams, a cousin from London. We really had a splendid evening and everybody is charmed with the court and its position. Mr Ford was in raptures over it and said, 'With a bit of winter rolling you'll have an absolutely perfect court here next year'.

He seemed to think that because the ground is level now, it must have 'growed' so, and said he can't imagine why we hadn't a tennis court there years ago! Slip, slop, splash!!! Very nice too!!! Well, that was Thursday. Friday afternoon mother went over to Knowle and I started the rather tall job of transforming my evening dress into a Sunday gown. In the evening, Antony and I went to church.

Yesterday afternoon I went to Pigeon House and Ant. came after tea, also Dick and Edie and we had quite a jolly time. Their tennis court is not very special yet, but we managed to get a bit of fun nevertheless.

Monday. When I reached this point I had to get the dinner and thought I'd finish the letter in the afternoon, but that little Pearce boy walked in while I was putting myself smart and as, of course, I had to look after him, there was little time for anything else. It is evident that when folks on the 'Defiance' have had enough of him, they politely offer him a day off! The grub seems rather pleased with himself and all the world. Work going fine! He is ever so much better than he was and can say a <u>whole sentence</u> without hesitation, but when he came up from hospital, he could hardly put 2 words together without stammering and stuttering. Seemed all nerves!

Mother tells me to put her post-script which is as follows: Mr Pearce came up last evening to 'fetch Alfred' and he said that a friend of his met him outside the Lord Mayor's Chapel and walked home with him and in the course of conversation asked him how Alfred was. Mr Pearce said, 'He's very well now; he's gone up to Fillwood this afternoon', and the other said, 'Oh, I know, I went to Fillwood with some peacocks when I was a little chap'. Dad immediately said, 'Was his name Budd?' and Mr P. said it was. The peacock in the hall is the one he brought here!! Rather queer, eh?

Ida is paying a short visit to Highridge and we are expecting her up here today for a game of tennis, also Clifford! Annie Milward has invited herself for the evening too!

I had a letter from Horton this morning, in which he mentioned that he had spent 3 hours in writing a letter to you. I don't know what on earth he could have written about - should rather like to know! Mrs Hitchen said in a letter to us that Horton's holiday here was the best he had ever had. While writing to him she said that Miss Williams enjoyed her stay at Fillwood more than any other part of her trip - America and all!!! What <u>wonderful</u> entertainers we must be!!!

Ah, well, I must once more, Adieu. Heaps of love and best possible wishes from your loving sister, Dor.

Horton Hitchen was a New Zealander - a friend of Mary Webb. His letter read:

HMS Druid, 1.6.15

Dear Syd,

I have just had a letter from Dorothy and as they sent me your address I will try and write you a bit of a letter, though there will not likely to be much news in it. How do you like your job at the Dardanelles? It will be a lot of change from what you were at this time last year. You went part of your journey on the 'Ayrshire', I heard. If so, did you ever meet George Kidd, the 2nd Refrigeration Engineer, or Jim Porch, the 4th Engineer? They were on while I was on her and we put in some pretty good times at different places.

You may have a chance of meeting Herbert out here as I have heard from home that he has joined up with some of the N.Z. contingent and was in camp at Petone getting a putting through. Have you been through much scrapping yet and what do you think of it so far? How is the place off for mosquitoes at night?

I was over at Fillwood a few days before you left England, so didn't get a chance to see you then, but hope to run across your path later on. I had a letter from Mary Webb last week and she was saying the Zeps passed over their house two times last visit, but did not drop anything on them. Mrs Page is getting a bit stronger now, but is still very weak yet, having been under an operation lately.

I had a letter from home (NZ) the other day (the first since November) and they were saying that Cass Williams is getting much better now. I suppose you know she was very ill and not expected to live, having caught a severe chill after an attack of ptomaine poisoning. She took bad after leaving Ceylon and on reaching NZ was confined to bed for some months. She was saying that the time they spent at Fillwood was the most enjoyable of the whole trip and that she would like to go back there again. I had a fine time there and was very sorry when Sunday night came along and it was time to make for the train.

How do you think you would like to live out in the Dardanelles or Egypt? I suppose you gave some of the Kan-Kan dancers a look up in Egypt, eh? Well, to tell you the truth, Syd, this is the damdest country I have ever had the misfortune to set eyes on so far and I can't make out why some people (writers etc.) refer to it as 'Dear old England'.

Have you run across many of the NZ chaps so far? Nearly all my mates are at the Dardanelles in the Otago and Auckland (NZ) divisions, and I wish I was there also and not buggering about here doing nothing but get fat. One thing, this climate seems to agree with me, as when I left Aus. I was 10 stone 1¼ lb, and now I must be over 11 stone. Well, I suppose you heard I joined the navy at London and got sent down to the Chatham Barracks. After six weeks there I was sent on a destroyer and have been there ever since. The pay is not so bad for this country, with extra given for destroyers, making it up to about 43 shillings a week.

I have only joined up for the duration of the war so the sooner it stops the better. We were allowed out every night at Chatham until 7am next day, so you can take it for granted we put in some pretty good times while there. Well, Syd, I will have to stop now and there is nothing I can think to say at present, so when you write, don't forget to put in all the news going and make a long letter of it.

Wishing you the very best of luck and a safe return home again. I remain, Yours to a cinder, Tanakgua. Kia-ora. H.H.H.

Sydney's letter of 22nd May to his father arrived on 10th June and Dor, vexed by his cryptic reference to the progress of the Gallipoli war, wrote back immediately, complaining that:

... in reality we know practically nothing beyond the fact that the landing was very difficult and the Allies have been steadily gaining ground, and it is rumoured that the Straits will soon be forced. Beyond this rather unsatisfactory information, nothing is published and I must say your letters do not give the censor cause to blunt his pencil! Can't you manage to give us a bit more news of what you are doing?

We were glad to hear that your 'interior' was proof against the water, but it is not surprising. All the fellows have not been trained with my celebrated cakes as you have! As to the sweets we sent, we've been expecting for a long time to hear that you've had them - the Easter cakes too - as we have wanted to send more, but have been afraid you'd not get them if you didn't get the others. However, I have made some coconut ice today and it and some chocs will be sent on spec.

THE STORMING OF THE GALLIPOLI CLIFFS: A MAGNIFICENT EXPLOIT.

AUSTRALIAN AND NEW ZEALAND BAYONETS CLEARING THE WAY AT GABA TEPE: THE HEROIC DASH WHICH MADE GOOD THE ARMY'S FOOTING.

WHERE THE DEFEATED TURKS WERE DRIVEN HEADLONG: THE STEEP GORGE DOWN WHICH THE DEFENDERS OF THE BEACH FINALLY FLED.

'The Illustrated London News', July 3, 1915

We were surprised to find no mention of Dennis Gough in your letter, as yesterday morning we had a letter from his mother saying that you two boys had met. How pleased you both must have been! Mother hopes to pay Mrs Gough a visit next week, so there will be some comparing of notes!

Bishopsworth was honoured yesterday by a visit from the Lord Bishop, who went to the schools, then to see the sick of the parish; back to tea at the vicarage, where the communicants were invited to meet him at 6.30pm. Of course, we turned out in our numbers and back to a service in church at 8 o'clock. The bishop is very nice indeed; we like him better on the vicarage lawn than in church.

Mother, Dad and I walked down, but Antony cycled and put his bike in at the Russells [Church Farm]. After we had been home some time, poor old Ant came in terribly hot, after having walked home! After church he went to get his bike, but it was minus, and the Russells having vowed that they knew nothing of it, he went down to the police station and left a description. Mr Parsons, our new bobby, has been up tonight and says the missing bike is where it was left, and was merely hidden, not stolen, so you see young folk still have their fling as of yore. Mr Jim Russell is very ill and has been for a considerable time, but he still goes to market etc. and seems just as keen on the business.

The event of the season is drawing perilously near; Dick's banns are to be published on Sunday next, for the first time, so the wedding is evidently not far distant. Perhaps it will be on July 8th, his 22nd birthday!

Lucy is to meet Edie and Floss in town tomorrow, so probably the gown will be bought. I should think Lucy and Floss will be bridesmaids, but what about Nell? One hears very little of her nowadays.

Ida was here this morning. She stayed at Highridge Farm Saturday to Wednesday, when she went to Pigeon House, and is coming here to stay a few days tomorrow. She says she has written to you twice since you went, so I hope you've had the letters.

Tomorrow Antony and I are due at a tennis party at the vicarage and, having had a letter from Alfred to say he would probably be up again for the weekend, I asked the vicar and his wife (much like my cheek) if they would mind him coming down in the evening. They will be <u>delighted</u>, so they say, and all that, as they are both <u>so fond</u> of him, so Mrs Ford says!!! Another Aunt!!!!

Something has happened to George Snook, but what it is seems to be a mystery. The first rumour said that he <u>had his hand or arm blown off</u>, then came the news that he had lost <u>some fingers</u>, the latest we have hard is that <u>one finger is gone or split</u>, and he's in hospital! Evidently, though, the first reports were somewhat exaggerated, and a good job too.

Mother and Dad have gone to Slimbridge today, paying their visits before the harvesting commences. We are all well; Mother was at Win's on Tuesday and she was A1, but Willie has a fearful cold and cough. He was so bad at night that it kept the neighbours awake ...

I think Mother and Dad will call there on the way from the station. Clifford has been up this evening. He is getting quite a crack tennis player and tonight he and Ant have been playing singles. Goodbye and good luck, Love from Dor.

From Alfred Pearce:

Mess 9, HMS Defiance, Devonport, 13.6.15

My dear Syd,

I have at last summoned up sufficient energy to write. I was very glad to know that you are getting on so well. I arrived in Bristol on Friday evening for a week-end spree. Went up to Fillwood on Saturday. The first thing then to do was to read the Admiralty report of your having been wounded. Then Dor and I drove to the vicarage. Dor went in to play tennis. I drove on to Highridge and had tea. Everyone there seems to be in the best of health.

After tea 'Aunty' Mab and I walked over to the vicarage. 'Aunty' would not play, but I did. the party broke up at about 8.20 and we three strolled back to Highridge for supper. We eventually reached Fillwood about 10 o'clock. There was a letter from you giving an account of your adventures. That allayed a good deal of anxiety.

The weather up here is simply glorious. Few people have started cutting yet. Murphy and Mr Gardiner are the only ones that I have seen with anything down. By the way, I partnered the delightful Lucy in one set. She was falling all over me, racquet, net and everyone and thing else about.

Dick's banns were called in church this morning. I have just returned from church with Dad and shall get 'up the hill' in time for tea. Have had one or two games on the new court. It is simply great.

Mother is screaming to me to have dinner, so I shall have to bid thee farewell. Am sending you on a box of smokes etc. Hope you receive 'em all OK.

Keep cool, my boy, and don't consume too much of the sand which is there. Drop me a line if poss. Much love, Thine, Alfred.

From Clara Hall:

Fillwood, Bishopsworth, June 12 1915

My very dear boy,

Dor sent a letter to you by Alf [Pitman] this morning and within half an hour we received a letter from the Admiralty (dated 10th June) to say Sergt. Sydney Llewellyn Hall had been slightly wounded in action near the Dardanelles, but has since been able to rejoin his unit for duty. You will know how anxious we shall be to have further news and I hope you'll not fail to give us details. I sincerely hope you will escape any further casualty. Have the Division generally suffered much? I hope not. How glad I shall be when this dreadful war is over. The news is not very cheerful I must say; we almost dread the post and the paper!

We had what might have been a bad accident yesterday, but luckily nobody and nothing was hurt. Going from Corby Street to Slimbridge in a 'tub', the pony shied at a donkey (silly ass, you'll say), and swerved to the hedge, where was a deep ditch into which pony, tub and we gently landed. The man who was driving got out quickly and at Dad's bidding, held the pony down to keep her from struggling. Flo Morgan and I got out behind, then Dad and he began unbuckling all the harness, by which time a neighbour on a bike rode up and helped. Then they pushed back the trap - free of horse and harness and got the pony out; then lifted the trap up, harnessed up and went on.

Poor Mrs Morgan was terribly frightened, but that was the worst happening and we were all very thankful. I bent my gown a bit and coming home from Knowle hitched my best coat on barbed wire. This wound up an eventful day! Despite these little 'pricks' we had altogether a pleasant time! Called at Win's. She was well, but Will had had three sleepless nights with dreadful cough. I saw him in town this morning and he is better.

I am sending a parcel on Monday. Do tell me if you want anything, and <u>what</u> you want, otherwise I must send haphazard! We all send love and hope you are well again and will get no further casualty, 'cause we want you home again, all in one piece, mind. Am going to see Mrs Gough next week. Your loving Mother.

Kind regards to Sergeant Ball - we all feel some interest in him from his likeness to you! Do you still have a sergeants' mess?

From little Ida Withers

Fillwood, Bishopsworth, Bristol

Dear Syd,

You will see by the above address that I am staying in Bishopsworth - only till today, though. Auntie Clara received your letter last night and was glad to see your accident was no worse, hope it is quite better by now. Auntie and Antony are just off to church, so Dorothy and 'my little self' are left to cook the dinner. I expect I shall do more reading. Dorothy wishes she could send you today's dinner. It is going to be something special but I must not let you know what it is or your mouth might get out of shape.

Many people have started hay-making, but the crops are very light this year. We have had no rain for quite a time now. Yesterday Dorothy and Antony (also that dear little man called Alfred) went to Mr Ford's for a game of tennis. We have a nice lot of black cherries this year; it is rather a long way to send you some, so I think you had better order a double share for when you come home.

Ernest Withers is home for the week-end - he has not left England yet. George Snook is in hospital somewhere in France; he has had a finger shot off. I think Edith and Dick's banns are to be called today for the first time. Cannot think of any more news. So goodbye, with much love (all to yourself) from Ida.

From Win:

June 16th 1915

My dear Syd,

How goes the world with you? Have you quite got over your wound? Saw your name in the Daily Mail yesterday; but of course had heard before from the War Office, and also by letter from you, so were not frightened. I hope that is the worst that will happen to you.

We have been hearing wonderful rumours lately that the Dardanelles have been forced; but nothing has got into the papers yet. I wonder who starts these reports; is it you?

Mother has gone to see Mrs Gough today to talk over 'fings' and is coming back here to stay the night. Mrs G. wrote and told me that you and Dennis had met - both possessing beards. How on earth did <u>you</u> manage to grow one? Not many hairs, I know. It must be only an apology.

It is rotten writing letters when there is no news and I don't know anything of interest to tell you. You need not trouble to write to me direct, for I see all the letters you send home, almost as soon as they do, but suppose I shall not see them quite as easily in the day now that the haymaking has started.

Well, old chap, be as good as you can, and mind you keep that beard in good order.

With fondest love from Will and Win.

From Dorothy:

Fillwood, Bishopsworth. June 17th 1915

My dear Syd,

Thank you very very much for your kindness in wishing to give me a new racquet, but though I much appreciate the offer, I do not intend to accept it just now for more reasons than one. In the first place, I bought a new one this year and it answers my purpose very well. You see, now haymaking is on the go, we shall not be playing much for a bit, and in any case it won't be tournament play!

Then again, if I were buying a good racquet, I should like to have a whole season's play with it before putting it away for the winter, when even the best ones are in danger of 'springing'. Just finish up this war and come home before the year is out and <u>then</u> I'll see how your pockets are lined!!! We shall all feel more like spending money when our boys are home again!

I believe Alf has written an account of the tennis party at the vicarage last Saturday. I had a ripping time, with very little rest, and very good partners. Miss Taylor is staying there for an unknown time and she is a splendid player, for a <u>female</u>! The vicar is in his usual fine form, Lucy is much better than usual. Mab has not started playing this year, though she came on the farm to watch, and it is doubtful if she will play now, as Auntie is expected home again next week. They are having a trained nurse with her, so we all hope the venture may be a success. For some time there has simply been a depression and a longing to get home, so it's <u>possible</u> it may do the trick! Let's hope so!!!

Mother and Auntie Lizzie went to see Mrs Gough yesterday afternoon and the former returned to Win's for the night. Antony has gone over there with eggs etc. this evening, so I suppose they'll come home together.

Mr Ford saw your letter containing news of your special shell(!) and was very much interested - then thanked me again and again for showing it to him, and yesterday Mr 'Jelly Bear' [de la Bere] and his 'Chief of Staff', Mr Longridge, came up and read that and your last letter to Dad. Now I had to explain your allusion to the former grub [de la Bere] who wished he could have seen my humorous report [on the visit with the vicar of Redcliffe to Fillwood], so I said I had told you about our game of tennis and <u>other things</u> and he took your address saying that he thinks he will send a report of his side of the question! The St John's school children are coming up in two batches (they number about 1,000 - without the infants) on July 3rd and July 10th - two Saturdays - so we've got something to look forward to!

Sunday School summer outing to Fillwood Farm from St John's, Bedminster

Yesterday morning Mother had a very nice letter from Dr Thomas, who had seen your name in the wounded list in one of the London papers. Mention was made that you had rejoined your unit. I don't know if it will come out in the T & M ['Bristol Times & Mirror'], but sincerely hope that is the worst news of you that they will be able to publish, and we won't grumble at that, for, of course, it brands you a hero! Hip, hip, hooray!!! George Snook's wound is a smashed finger and seems to have happened in the nick of time to get him home for the wedding, which is to take place at Portbury on July 8th - Dick's birthday. Mr Ford to perform the ceremony and Floss and Lucy will be bridesmaids. I hope to be able to tell you more later, as I've been invited to Glenmere the day before to see the thing through!!

Antony went down there with Ida on Sunday last, returning Monday evening, and on Tuesday morning Charlie, Lil and Ruth appeared here to buy a cow! Our godchild certainly <u>does</u> us credit so far(!), for she's a sweet little kiddie.

Next Monday we are expecting the advent of the Rev. and Mrs Theodore Page, so we'll have to put on best behaviour.

Mother and Antony have returned from Knowle and it's getting towards supper time. The men had lunches for the first time today, so work is on the go. Dad has bought a new side delivery rake too! We didn't send the coconut ice I had made, thinking hard drops might arrive in better condition.

Au Revoir. Hope you are quite well, Much love, from Dor.

His mother added:

June 17, 1915

My dear boy,

Returned from Knowle and had supper, but must add a few lines to put in with Dor's letter. We were all so delighted to get your letter and to know the wound so far caused so little inconvenience. I hope it was healed by this time and that it will be the worst of your experiences.

We had a delightful time with Mrs Gough who gave us a most hearty welcome, strawberries and cream for tea and news of her son. She said he was relieving you in your trench, so I am wondering if you will be often meeting him!

I called at the Babers on the way home. Gladys Clarke is to be married most probably on Saturday week, 26th, to Lieut Sydney Morgan [?] who is on leave from France for breakdown. The wedding is to be very quiet.

I forgot to say, Mrs Gough has left Chesterfield Buildings and is living in a flat in Tyndalls Park Road. Every comfort of course!

You will be interested to know that Clara Cox and old Mrs Howe enquired for you last Sunday. The latter declares she believes you saved her life; she shall always think so!! What a happy thought for you!

Yesterday I posted a parcel to you - sweets, laces, boracic powder and Keating's [insecticide powder] - shall send an old shirt next week. It will be something clean for you if you can't get your underclothes washed. Do tell me anything we can send that will be useful. Now I know you've had one parcel, I shall have hope in sending others. Do you want soap? I'll send some next time.

Now I must be off to bed - feathers tonight, not mattress - <u>not cold ground</u>, poor boy. When oh when will you be able to have such a luxury again - feather bed, I mean! Much love, dear boy, and good luck attend your efforts. Your loving Mother.

From Baghot de la Bere:

June 15, 1915

My Dear Sydney,

Having read a good many of your more recent letters, I sometimes feel I ought to write to you an answer, not that I have a great deal to say. <u>You</u> have the news, and most interesting it is to hear all you tell of your experiences. You are up against a stiff job in the Dardanelles. I think most of us at home are beginning to realize it, in spite of the absurd optimism of Mr Churchill at Dundee. But I dare say you don't often see the daily papers and don't take much note of what you read therein. Your time and thoughts are well occupied.

I go up to Fillwood occasionally. I wish it were a little oftener, for it is a peaceful and beautiful spot and your folk always give me such a jolly welcome. On Sat. July 3rd I am taking a gang of Sunday School children up there to have tea and play in the field. I am afraid the haymaking will be over, or we might have helped.

In the country, in the midst of our most beautiful English summer, it takes quite an effort of the imagination to picture the horror of war; and indeed it is good to forget sometimes, for it serves more often to stress the mind, and of course it comes home to me from day to day in hearing of the loss of life from among one's friends or parishioners and neighbours. It is an awful business - sometimes one just feels what fools we must seem to the angels, to be fighting as we do instead of staying peacefully at home in our countries. Of course, there is some consolation in saying to the Germans, 'You began it' and there is more consolation in the thought that if we had not gone to war last August, the Germans would in all probability have been in England by now. At any rate we regard the fallen with unmixed admiration and gratitude. You are fighting for great causes - for home and freedom, for God and righteousness. God grant it may be a war that shall end war.

I know from your letters that you are prepared to live and die for your country, and you could do nothing better with your life. 'Greater love hath no man than this, that he may lay down his life for his friends'.

However, I hope if God so wills, to meet you once again when your work is done, under the paternal roof beam of Fillwood Farm. Mind I don't expect an answer to this, for I know how difficult letters are and I hear from others all about you. But I thought you might like a word from one who is proud to be numbered among your friends.

God bless and keep you. Your affectionate friend, Baghot de la Bere.

'Auntie' Langford, who had billeted Sydney and others when he was stationed at Deal, wrote (undated):

St Clare Lodge, Upper Walmer

Dear Mr Hall,

Just to let you know we have not forgotten, but are still interested in the welfare of the RNDDE. It seemed a long time before we heard any news of you at all, but can now follow your doings by the paper.

We were sorry to see the loss of your youngest Lt. and that Lt. Marshall and Lt. A.H. Roe were also wounded, and the latter so soon after his promotion. Then in today's list I saw Corpl. Dines is seriously wounded and also your name, but was thankful to see only slightly and now rejoined unit.

But such is warfare, and what a terrible war it is - some will come through it, while others fall. We trust that the three chums may be preserved and return to their friends and homes when peace is restored.

There have been several air raids, one coming very near to us - dropping bombs at Okney Bottom, in a field and mercifully passing over Walmer and Deal to Ramsgate, where considerable damage was done and three persons killed.

We often talk about you all and Walmer seems quite deserted now; we are pleased to have the photos of you all. The choir at St Mary's is composed of boys, only 2 men now and often but one. Last Sunday an old member was there - Sgt Wincole. Walmer is looking very pretty just now. I expect you long sometimes for a sight of its freshness.

Please give our kind regards to any of the NCOs who may be near you, and sympathy to those who are sick and wounded. It was reported you would be returning shortly, but we think it hardly likely to be true. With sincere wishes for your welfare and safety,

Yours sincerely, A.W. and E.S. Langford.

From Antony:

June 20th, 1915

Dear Syd,

Once more I give up my afternoon's nap to write to you. It seems only a fortnight ago since I wrote, but about a week ago somebody received a letter saying you wanted some more lies and rot, so I suppose it is longer ago than I thought. I should have written last Sunday, but for the fact that Ida W. was here and had to go home, so Mother told me to go with her, to keep her out of mischief (not my own free will).

By the way, I had to use your bike as mine has been stolen; the facts are these: Thursday week his Reverence the Bishop of Bristol came to B'port [Bishport was an older name for Bishopsworth], and as my pump had disappeared at Church House about a week previously, I went there to get it before going to the Vicarage. Having got it, I thought it was not worthwhile to cycle round and back again, so I left my bike in the greenhouse. When I returned it was missing. Naturally I blamed the girls and when they said they knew nothing about it, I tried to get them to give it up by telling them I should let the policeman find it. Howsomever, I couldn't get it, so the policeman will (if he has not already), but I have found out since that it was Harry who did it without letting the girls know, so I shall get it some day, but they will not see me there again, I'm afraid.

Dad bought a new side rake on Wednesday but as we've only used it on Rudges up to now, can't say how it will work. Sam Bellamy has left school and will be a useful kid, I expect. We have done all but about 4 acres of the clover and got the small side of Homemead cut, so we are getting on with it.

I hear Ernie Withers has a fortnight's leave for haymaking. I should like you to see that young 'Whipper-Snapper' (as you once called him). Conceit is not a strong enough term for'n, he is too proud to shake with me now. Leslie C----r also is getting a lot too big for his clothes; he called Dad and Mr B-----y bastards and rogues for letting some of Murphy's sheep get through his fence into his mowing grass. Never mind, my day will come, sooner or later, and the last to laugh etc. etc.

Miss Chapman (that was) is coming tomorrow. I'll give her your love. Excuse mistakes, bad writing etc. Ever thine, Antony.

From Mother:

June 20 1915

My dear Sydney,

[after apologising for the delay in writing occasioned mostly by social calls all Sunday]

Dad and I have been up round the fields since tea - barley looking very well, and wheat good. Potatoes and roots doing nicely. Clover will, I think, be finished tomorrow morning (if time) and there is every prospect of it; then they will be in Homemead and if this fine weather continues, our hay harvest will be soon over.

We had green peas for dinner today, but the beef which cost 1/- a lb. was rather tough and we shall be glad to cook some of our old hens this year. They are worth 2/9 so I hear! Chicken 4/- and 4/6 each! So you see grub is decidedly dear nowadays! Perhaps it's lucky I've lost a front tooth - shall have to live on soft food!!! Till I get a new top set, I suppose.

Grace and Sidney were at church this morning - both looking well. Grace had a pretty blue dress which suited her! Marriages still going strong. After Dick's banns this morning (2nd time) came Jack Reynolds with Anne Mathias! Joe Verbyst collected! I fancy he will be married this week, but don't know where they'll live.

Saw Amy this morning. They are fetching a trained certificated nurse from Keynsham tomorrow and Auntie Sarah comes home on Tuesday. Dr. Butterford has advised a trial and told them if any difficulty arose at any time to apply to him at once, but he quite thinks the trial will be successful.

THE CAMPAIGN IN THE DARDANELLES:
SLOW BUT SURE PROGRESS ON THE ROAD THAT LEADS TO CONSTANTINOPLE

OUR HEAVY ARTILLERY IN ACTION: SHELLING ONE OF THE FORTS ON THE GALLIPOLI PENINSULA

BETWEEN THE DEVIL AND THE DEEP SEA: HOW THE AUSTRALIANS CORNERED A TURKISH DETACHMENT

Progress in Gallipoli is to be measured rather in the number of Turks killed than in the number of yards we have advanced. According to Sir Ian Hamilton's report, the enemy's casualties during four days of last week amounted to 20,000, the ground in front of the trenches being covered with dead as far as the eye could reach.

SKETCHES BY ARTURO BIANCHINI, OUR SPECIAL ARTIST AT THE DARDANELLES

Optimistic reporting in 'The Graphic', July 10, 1915

Jean wrote the other day for your address. She wants to send you a parcel. Please tell me what you really would like sent, because whoever sends parcels may as well send what is most acceptable - failing what you <u>want</u> ...

Clara Cox enquired very kindly for you this morning! I hear Percy Hooper has joined 'Bristol's Own'. May and Stanley were here last night. Stanley looks very well, but feels weak in back and gets headaches! He hopes to get further leave, otherwise he returns next week.

I expect Son has told you all his news and as I am going to put his letter in with mine, you'll have enough to read. Much love dear Boy, and best wishes for your welfare - from us all.

Your loving Mother.

PS. Sorry you've got such a bother to cook your grub - hard lines when you get plenty to cook.

From Ronald Warne, Sydney's old friend, formerly of Great Custon, Wheeler's Wood, above Lower Knowle Farm, Knowle.

The Hermitage, 16 Henleaze Road, Westbury-on-Trym, Bristol, June 20 1915

Dear Syd,

Just had a card from Dor to say you had been hit but on the whole are getting on quite well. Glad to hear it's nothing serious and hope the next time you see shrapnel coming you won't try to stop it with your body.

How are things going with you? All right, I hope, mind and keep fit, and if there's anything you want (cigarettes etc.) just drop me a card and I'll send it on.

I don't think I've much news I can tell you. Maud Horler and Bill Ringham - do you remember them - have got engaged and are still in the heavenly heights that happy state usually sends people. Hope they'll be happy, but they both have queer dispositions, and myself am rather doubtful.

Ernie Egbester, Len Moore and Frank Ringham have all got commissions. Frank is somewhere in the north of England and the amount of work he is doing may be judged from the fact that he wired for his tennis racket and golf clubs! They seem to get an easy time in the Junior Service.

Bristol's Own (12th Gloucesters) still remain at Ashton Gate and are heartily sick of the place and are all longing to get to France. Yours truly has visited the dentist and lost 9 teeth in the adventure. But guess it didn't hurt as much as shrapnel, eh? However, he's recovering now.

I expect Dor has told you that I am now a full blown Scoutmaster to a troop of 40 Scouts. Swank! Have had some very interesting times and also some most humorous ones. Will get you to give them a lecture on 'How I was hit in the seat of the trousers at the Dardanelles by the Nasty Turk' when you get home.

By the way, are you learning Turkish? It might be useful. In any case, just learn the way to make Turkish Delight and Turkish cigarettes - the only two decent things that ever came from Turkey that I've heard of. Hope the censor won't maul this about, it's really too brilliant to be blue-pencilled!!! I expect he's a kind man however, and will spare it as much as possible (I put that bit in just to blarney him over, you know).

Believe tennis is progressing favourably at Fillwood. Hope to go over one evening, but am so full up (<u>not</u> with food) that I don't get very much time.

Saw the beautiful and accomplished <u>Miss</u> *Lucy the other day on College Green. And - horror - she cut me (no, not with a knife - Editor). I hope you are not forgetting her manifold charms whilst basking in the sunshine of the lovely eyes of the Turkish ladies. I suppose they are lovely - or do they eat garlic like all fat Turkish fathers?*

Well, Lochinvar, I must close with a rider to the effect that I hope you will behave yourself and not get fighting unnecessarily.

With love from all, yours to a cinder, Ronald.

Ronald's brother, who signed himself 'M II' wrote Sydney a postcard (undated) about this time:

Dear old Sid,

I wonder where you are, how you are? We often talk of you. Ron had 5 teeth out Sat. week. Just had a line from Penelle - he said all the Devons were sitting in their Hut at Bently Essex, singing 'Devon, Glorious Devon', 'How's that' and 'I just come up from Somerset'. Ron and I motored to Portishead to see to the camping of the Scouts. Mr Ringham married again. Maud and Will still chums. Essie has a corn. Eddie still sitting on a store at War Office.

Since becoming Sergeant Major, Sydney's pocket book is full of Company Returns, recording who in each Section was fit for duty, detailed for special duties, who was sick at HQ, in hospital or wounded - the numbers daily brought up to date so that he could at any time report to his superiors on the strength of his Company. There are returns of missing helmets, lists of materials needed for entrenching and details of instructions issued to each Section. There is not much room or time for personal observations, though on 14th June he wrote:

Company working on communications. Each section taking a working party, 3 per 24 hours. Wound healing but boils. Job going smoothly, improving camp. No disturbing elements except flies and rumours of impending commission.

On June 23rd he wrote to his sister Win. With his new responsibilities, his spirits were high:

June 23 1915

Dear Win,

I've got ever so much to say, so where shall I start? Shall I say how well I am, which is very, or how d'ye do, which I 'as 'igh 'opes of; or shall I describe the chronological order of events in this period of entity? The night I wrote my last letter, whimpering because the mails were disordered, I got a letter from Dor. No doubt she meant well in informing me in such a curious way of the impending [nuptials?] of Miss Lucy Withers, but her true intent for my delight was baulked by Ida of that ilk, whose letter got here 2 days before. Her other topic, the parson, certainly has enjoyed some attention lately, it seems he knows the way to go ...

He acknowledges receipt of letters from all the rest of the family:

Some mail, and very cheerful reading I find it.

The Sergeant Major has been carrying out his duties in a modest and bashful way, and incidentally healing his infirmities. The wounds have gone, but an ebullition of eruptions where the plaster was placed, still excites ennui, making it absolutely advisable to proceed placidly, or feel before you flop. Otherwise he's doing well and just at present, more or less content with his lot, or he's anticipating dinner. After, and jolly good too! There is now a canteen established here and the little delicacies we can get here occasionally tend to make meals merry and bright, I tell myself, and notice particularly among the men now 'bread strengthens man's heart'.

We have had considerable sickness, but the general health is now much better, thanks to the canteen and three day's comparative rest. This paper was bought at the canteen. We tried a new feeding scheme today, viz. bread and cheese at midday and meat rations at evening. It seemed to work well and I hope by much wangling and careful sanitation, to circumvent the flies against which I have sworn to wage by force or guile, eternal war.

I won't talk about the campaign, you will know more than I now do - but prospects seem rosier. I had a hint from Willie of current events and all I can do is to offer my best, very best wishes to the firm of Will, Win and Co.

It is now getting late and darkness soon increases here, so that is enough excuse for me, so with best love to all from Syd, I will introduce the Finis.

From Win to Syd:

June 23 1915.

My dear Syd,

Just a line to let you know we are still in the land of the living and hope you are. I saw your note yesterday to mother. Am so sorry you are in such a plight and the flies worry you so much. They <u>are</u> beastly things with a vengeance. How are your wounds now? Poor old mother is so upset about them. She <u>does</u> wish you could come home so much, and so say all of us.

As far as I can hear, haymaking is getting on finely. We have had the first rain today for about 6 weeks, am not sure if that is quite the time, but it is somewhere near it. What a difference a drop of rain makes.

Have you heard that Mr Lloyd George is now Minister of Munitions? He has been to Bristol and in fact to most large towns. He is without a doubt a most wonderfully clever man and is doing ever such good work. Everyone seems to have changed their opinions of him.

Well Syd, I have not any news, but still I feel I must write to you. Oh, by the way, Dad came here the other day from town <u>in his shirt sleeves</u>. You may guess I was surprised to see him like that coming swanking through this aristocratic neighbourhood! Mother said one consolation was the shirt was clean. How's the beard?

With fondest love, Will and Win.

From Dorothy:

June 24th 1915

Congratulations (or sympathies?) on your promotion and best wishes for future success.

My dear Syd,

In my last letter to you I said that we didn't mind the wound you had had, if you didn't get anything worse, but we thought it was very slight and did not imagine it was going to fester or anything of that sort! Allow me to inform you that we <u>do</u> mind that and hope it's quite alright now. Mr Ford has suggested that it sounds rather bad to say you were wounded in the <u>back</u>,

The DIFFICULTIES of the DARDANELLES.

Miles of Barbed Wire Supported by Metal Poles with Jagged Tops all Along the Cliff Tops

The Turko-German forces on the peninsula guarded every possible place with barbed-wire entanglements, strung between wooden and metal poles. The heads of the latter were found to be finished off with a serrated edge to make the passage of the barrier still more difficult

The Actual Condition of Seddul Bahr Fort After Much Bombardment

This view shows how much pounding these old forts will take without becoming level with the ground. The end on the right pointing seawards has naturally caught the fire worst, but the flanking wall still stands

More realistic reports in 'The Sphere', June 12, 1915

being an Englishman! Only the fact that you have been promoted saves you from disgrace. Judging from your report, your abode of rest was not all that could be desired; so I hope you hadn't long to <u>enjoy</u> it.

A righteous war is being waged here on the fly tribe and judging from the number of carcasses stuck to the window panes, it looks as if the members of the household often feel spiteful on your account! As a matter of fact, the common houseflies are not as worrying this year as usual, but blue-bottles are here in abundance - a bigger squash every time a murder is committed! How do you like the warm weather? S'pose you have some!

Dad has finished the clover - two mows - and Home Mead is well on the way and the best crop anywhere about here! I have not personally inspected the plough grounds during the last few weeks, but hear splendid reports of their prosperous looks. Dad is delighted with wheat and barley up to now and, as you know, there's quite a lot of it. The reaper has not been put in working order yet - but probably your enquiry may do the trick! The horses are looking quite well considering their work and Jerry is getting no milk cart pulling, except Sundays, as Antony and Sam go to Bedminster twice a day now - result - we get the paper about two hours earlier than heretofore - and other benefits!

Sam has left school and is on the 'Fillwood staff' and I expect a very useful little member. His grandfather was not well last Monday, though at work, and in the evening had to send for the doctor, who said he had strained his heart - poor old chap - I shouldn't think he'll do much more work - but then, how many times have we said that!

We beat everybody with our potatoes this year and all but the Vicar with green peas, having had two meals of them. I haven't heard a cuckoo for several days and the landrail <u>has</u> started his melodious turn. Now I think all your questions are answered, except one. 'Does anyone wish old Siddie were there?' Now you are fishing, and for being a good boy you shall get a bite. Yes, <u>I</u> do for one, and <u>if</u> nobody else wishes it, I think I do enough for them all - but I really and truly believe you would be a <u>very</u> welcome visitor to all! Ah, well, there's a good time coming!!!

Mr & Mrs Theodore Page arrived here on Monday evening; on Tuesday rested until the afternoon when Mrs Page and I went over to Win's for tea [and there follows a list of friends and neighbours who called], all but the Vicar and his niece, who only stayed a couple of hours as the pony had a colt at home! We had some games of tennis, but the court is very cracked for want of a drink.

This morning Mother has gone to town to buy a present for Dick - a little table, I expect, and a watch for you. She sent off a parcel containing paper and envelopes, pants, socks etc. today, so I hope you'll get it alright.

Mr Page is <u>very</u> quiet, but this is evidently not because he knows nothing, he was a chemist before entering the ministry and became B.Sc., and since has gained 'Bachelor of Divinity' and is studying for DD. Mrs Page is much thinner than of yore and seems very well pleased with her lot in life. They want mother to go to Cheddar with them one day - either Saturday or Monday. I hope she will.

Ernie Withers is home for a fortnight - to help with the haymaking. He had no difficulty getting it off. George Snook has not been home yet, but is in a convalescent home in Essex. Old Mr

Russell died yesterday after a long illness, so I suppose there will be a change at Church Farm again. Don't know what Dolly and Hepsy will do, but I should think they'll take situations.

Aunt Sarah is home once more, but I haven't heard how she is, and of course shall not go up to see! Bristol's Own left for camp at York yesterday, so are a step further towards the front. What will Miss Mallard do?

Heaps of love, hoping you are now A1. Your loving sister, Dor.

This was the last letter from home that Sydney is known to have received, for it was found among his possessions after his death. Undoubtedly others were written during the next three weeks, but owing to the time lag, they did not arrive until after he died and so were not preserved.

On July 8th, his father's birthday, he wrote:

Gallipoli, July 8th 1915

Dear Dad,

Here's a letter to you to show you I have remembered the old date and my present wish, which I suppose is dated July 8th and therefore correctly timed, is many and happy healthy returns to you. I am always thinking of what a jolly harmonious family I belong to, and pray that it may remain intact for many years to come. In other words, long live we! About the sincerest toast I ever composed.

After saying that I'm quite well, I'm now reduced to the old trick of commenting on the letters I've had. The last batch was dated June 11th to 13th and included one from Dor, one from Mother about the Slimbridge adventure, one from Alfred, one from Ida and one from Auntie Langford who billeted us NCOs at Walmer. A great mail, I suppose, partly due to the newspaper report of my wound. I'm glad it was so arranged so as not to give you anxiety; as a matter of fact, I hadn't expected it to be published at all. All is quite well.

Dor's letter tells me that you find difficulty in piecing up the scraps of information I have given you, so I will just make a short story of the general items. [Then follows a short resumé of his movements since leaving England up to the landing at Seddülbahir]. We've been hammering away at this job ever since, our work, since a definite line was established, being communicating, trench digging and maintenance and assisting in advance and construction of new fire trenches. A very monotonous job in a blazing climate is what our scientific and educated youths are come to, and it's pulled some of them about. It's not exciting at all, but we keep cheerful and look forward to a better time someday.

I didn't write details of the war; they're too sordid to speak of; so don't think I'm robbing you of anything worthwhile when I confine my letters to bosh and platitudes.

I met Gough again about a week ago and we had a good jaw. He's well, but had a slightly festered hand, so was down at the Field Ambulance for a day or two. He told me his Ma had written to Mother, but didn't you get my letter in which I described our previous meeting? Shame. I sent a beauty, as usual.

I am so glad to hear of your lucky escape at Slimbridge. Squeaks ain't confined to France or the Dardanelles. I hope all the Morgan families are A1, those at Tickenham and Bath.

Tell Alfred I had his letter and will reply someday, but that the Sergeant Major is sufficiently employed nowadays. I volunteered for extra work a few days ago and got it - now I'm doing my best to slip it again; another lesson learnt! Let sleeping dogs lie. Good Luck with the harvest; I shall be delighted to get a small box of the harvest apples in the orchard, something to chew! I miss apples more than anything else in the food line. Well, Dad, I've exhausted my paper, so will conclude with much love to all,

Your affectionate son,

Syd.

Shamelessly patriotic advertising in 'The Graphic', September 4, 1915

No. 1 Field Coy. Camp.   *Gall. Pen. 26 July, 1915*

Dear Mrs Hall,

I regret that the first communication that I have with you should be in regard to the sad death on duty of your gallant son and my Sergt. Major S.L. Hall. He was extremely popular with the men and his high character and abilities were much appreciated by all the officers. His loss is consequently both personal and one that we shall long be conscious of.

The circumstances of your son's death were briefly as follows. He went off on horseback after lunch on the 21st inst. (Wednesday last) to the base depot on the sea shore and soon after his arrival there, was struck on the head by a Turkish shell, and instantly killed. The horse was also mortally wounded, but bolted back towards the horselines for nearly a mile before falling dead at the roadside. Though the best medical skill was at once forthcoming, it was found that your son was beyond all human aid.

His funeral took place at 2.00pm the following day at the cemetery at Cape Helles, in all reverence and solemnity, and was attended by a representative squad of the Company.

Allow me in closing to express my very sincere sympathy with you in your terrible loss, and remain, Yours very truly, G.E. Morgan. Major O.C. No. 1 F.C.

The Hall family heard of Sydney's death, not from this letter, but from an official communication from Lieut Commander A. Randall Wells, RNVR, announcing his 'death from wounds received on May 28th'. This was received at Fillwood in the late afternoon of Wednesday.

Sydney's uncle, Edwin Wyatt, wrote in his almanac that day: 'Office till 1. Went with Gerald to Burnham. Fine. His weight 8.7. Afternoon - heard of S. Hall's death'.

To the further distress of the Hall family, Clara received a letter from Sydney the next day, dated July 16th.

Dear Mother,

Since I wrote last, I have had another mail of 6 letters, from you, Dor, Win, Son, Ronald and the Rev. de la Bere. It's great to get so much news and good wishes; but I feel quite unable to make adequate replies. Fact is, I'm in charge of 50 men and have to keep in touch with about 200 more, so I'm rather busy. All the fit men and officers are in the front trench and I'm in charge of the sick and details, as well as having to go to and from the others. Well, I'm absolutely recovered, and in good health.

And now for the letters. Am sorry to hear of Mr Russell's death. Son's escapades at Church House are over, I suppose. As regards bikes, Son can make use of mine, if he wants, of course; his must be pretty far gone by now. Ronald's letter of sympathy was rather more slushy than usual. Wrote that commissions are fairly cheap at home today. To evade common vulgarity, I think I'd better remain a Sgt Major; there's only one of them to 4 of the others, and I bet I'm the youngest S.M. in the army. I'm glad you've had such a lot of visitors of various sorts; quite a lively lot. Mrs Th. Page was a great pal of mine at one time, I believe. I remember when the grindstone was near the new stable door - hearing 'Archie! Sydney! Come in'. When I was less than 6 years, 1 week and 1 day.

Am so glad the harvest looks so promising, and hope the rain will come when required. I note all the marriages coming off and the news about all the boys at home. Stanley C., Ernie W., George S. and so on. I see from the paper that Cpl. W. Keel of Stockwood was wounded.

Mr de la Bere's letter was very kind and much appreciated. He says I shouldn't reply to him, but I think I should; so I won't. Which is a high compliment to his opinions, eh?

We seem to be in a position to keep moving forward at a price. I hope they'll pay it now, for it will be heavier if paid in instalments. This place is getting foul too; we want more land. So strike, strike, strike, be our motto.

I am so glad that shirts and socks have been sent. I could do with a new shirt every 6 weeks or so, and among other things, such goodies as cakes, apples and lollies would always be rapturously welcomed, but to come safely, they want to be well boxed up. Parcels take a month or 5 weeks to get here; beastly slow, I call it. But by Jove, aren't they appreciated when they come!

Am glad Auntie Sarah has come home again and I do sincerely hope she'll get well. Best love to one and all at the Common, am so glad my haymow was successful. I had enough advice in making that mow to run parallel for 6 months, so no wonder (or great wonder) that it's alright! It would be a business making hay here, with this sun you'd want a collector tied on the mowing machine. The flies are still very bad; but I don't expect they'll get any worse, and sincerely hope that we shall now escape the plague here.

I'd love to step round the corner into our dairy now; oh, wouldn't the cakes go, and the milk and cream, also the pies; likewise the apples, pears and plums, though they'd be rather unripe yet, I fear. Well, enough about my tummy's loves; poor old tummy must be good without such encouragements, but a good boy compared with some, anyway. Short end, extra superfine love, from Syd.

Clara Hall wrote to Lieutenant-Commander A. Randall Wells:

Sir,

Your communication announcing the death of my son Sgt Major Sydney Llewellyn Hall from wounds received on May 28th reached me last night. This morning I received a letter from him dated July 16th in which he says he had absolutely recovered and was in good health. May I hope there is some mistake in your communication?

Yours sincerely, Clara Hall.

But Major Morgan's letter which must have arrived a few days later, left no room for doubt. The feelings of the family may be imagined. If these were expressed - which is doubtful - in relaying the news to the many relations and friends, they have not survived. That Sydney did not expect to survive the war became clear to them when his pocket book and other possessions were returned to them. He had written inside the front cover:

In the event of my death, please forward this book and the contents of my pockets to Mr B. Hall, Fillwood, Bishopsworth, Bristol, England.

And on the last page he had written:

God bless Mother, Dad, Sisters, brother and all kind friends, and accept me a humble servant. Amen.

Even in that terrible year, when the death of so many young men was a daily occurrence, the sense of loss and shock must have been overwhelming. The main burden of correspondence fell inevitably on the practical Dorothy. She wrote to her cousin on the 6th:

My dear Margie,

No doubt you have heard the awful news that our dear Syd died on July 21st. We don't know the cause, but think he must have been killed in action. At any rate, it was not *from the old wounds as previously reported. That was a clerical mistake in the report.*

Can't stop for more. Mother and Dad are bearing it bravely, though of course, it's an awful blow. Your loving cousin, Dor.

The card and envelope were heavily bordered in black and must have been one of dozens she wrote that day. Next day she wrote by hand again to all the Halls announcing the memorial service. To Margie again:

Fillwood, August 7th 1915.

There is to be a memorial service at our Church tomorrow evening at 6.30. We thought, if fine, you might like to cycle up; or if only one comes, there's room and a welcome in my bed. I know it's not much good asking both to stay. If wet, of course, we shall not expect you. Love to all, Dorothy.

Uncle Edwin's diary: 'Aug. 8. School and service in mg. School afternoon. Serv in evg. Memorial Service for Sydney Hall at evg. service'.

Tributes poured in from all sides - the things said and unsaid upheld the Halls during these dark days. Among the letters of consolation, Clara preserved one or two.

From the Head of the Faculty of Engineering, Bristol University:

The Harbour House, Portmahomack, Ross-shire. 11 Aug. 1915

Dear Mr Hall,

I have been deeply affected by the news which has just reached me of your boy's death and I should like to send you my sincerest sympathy in your sad bereavement. Your son was a young man of great promise and I have followed his career closely and looked forward to seeing him a highly successful engineer. He had won the affectionate regard of those who taught him and worked with him.

We are proud of our young men who give their lives and fall in this terrible war and we, who can only look on, would not wish to hold them back from the great dangers which they go to face.

I hope you may have some definite news as to how your boy met his death; and that you and his mother may find comfort and consolation in his brave self-sacrifice.

Again with assurances of my deep grief and sympathy, Yours sincerely, John Munro.

('Answered 19.8.15' wrote Clara on the top of the letter).

From the Engineering Society:

13th October 1915.

Dear Sir,

At a recent meeting of our Engineering Society, the first of this session, it was unanimously resolved that we should write to express our heartfelt sympathy with you in the sad bereavement which you have sustained by the death of your son.

Those here who knew him recall him as a student of high principle and endeavour. He was a prominent member of the Society and contributed greatly to its success, both by his papers and by his helpful criticism. His great ability, and the keenness he displayed in everything he undertook, led us to expect great things for his future. The readiness with which he helped others appealed to us even more.

We are proud to remember him as one of us, and shall ever honour his memory.

I am, dear Sir, Yours very sincerely,

Frank H. Bullock (Honorary Secretary of the Society)

Cape Helles, where Sydney is buried, is a lovely spot. It is the extreme south-west tip of the Gallipoli peninsula, elevated, treeless, windswept, with two sides surrounded by 100-foot cliffs, and lying on a gentle slope which descends gradually to a saucer-like depression in the middle of the plateau. It is one of six war cemeteries on the Helles front and in the early days, before the Commonwealth War Graves Commission regularised it, it exhibited a miscellaneous collection of improvised crosses, some wood, some twisted metal, with name and rank painted somewhat crudely with white paint.

The cemetery at Cape Helles before it was regularised by the Commonwealth War Graves Commission. Sydney Hall's cross is indicated by the arrow

It is a measure of the regard for Sydney Hall among the men of the 1st Division that his grave was the only one to be commemorated with a headstone in the form of a massive Celtic cross, carved by a man from his own company and erected under continuous shellfire from the Asian shore. Sgt Alfred Ball, one of Sydney's NCOs and a close friend, made himself responsible for sending his personal possessions back to Fillwood.

Written in pencil:

The Gallipoli Peninsula, 12 Oct. 1915.

Dear Mrs Hall,

Your letter dated Aug. 26th reached me a few days ago - for which I thank you. I trust you have received the wristwatch long before this letter reaches you. I wrapped it carefully inside some underclothing which came in the same parcel and sewed the whole bundle strongly in a cloth. Lieut Mawson then put his signature to the parcel. I do hope it has reached you without damage.

As regards your son's treasures and diary, these are in all cases dealt with by the company clerk as part of his duty and I have no doubt but you have also received these by now. The man has left us, otherwise I would enquire of him.

I had the sorrowful task, and yet was pleased to perform the last token of respect, of erecting the cross over your son's grave. The cross was an excellent piece of work in white stone, about 3ft 6ins high, including the pedestal, and was made by a man in the company who is a stonemason in civilian life.

Sgt Alfred Ball

I have also made arrangements for a friend to photograph the grave and for you to have a copy. I trust my arrangements will get through satisfactorily and shall be glad if you will kindly inform me, at my home address: 'Roseneath', Sydenham Park Road, London SE, if you receive the photo safely.

Very best wishes and kindest regards, from yours very sincerely, Alfred J. Ball.

The photo was received and so was another, much larger, one of that part of the cemetery where it was situated. The family treasured these photographs, on the back of which Sgt Ball had written: 'Grave of Sgt Major S.L. Hall, 1st Field Company, R.N.D. Engineers. The stone was quarried and carved by Sapper Beach (of the above company) on the Gallipoli Peninsula and erected by a comrade in the cemetery above 'Lancashire Landing' at Cape Helles. It is certainly one of the finest tombstones erected in memory of our fallen heroes and friends on the Peninsula. A.J.B. July 21st 1915'.

The family were understandably distressed when this fine stone was later removed and replaced by the standardised War Graves Commission tablet in common with all the others. In the process the appearance of the cemetery was inevitably much altered. Within enclosing walls of sloping white stone, and spreading down the slope from the restrained and sombre altar step inscribed 'THEIR NAMES LIVE FOR EVER', the rows of tablets lie in attendant ranks of lavender and myrtle.

There is an indefinable sense of timelessness and peace in those Gallipoli war cemeteries. There is no noise in the peninsula today, only the rustling of the needles of the stunted pine trees and the distant throb of a Turkish tractor or reaper and the crying of wood pigeon. The thousands of names all have stories to tell, like that of Sydney Hall. Most of the tablets give only the briefest detail - name of Company and Division, place of enlistment and number, name, rank, age and date of death.

There is room below for a personal message from the bereaved families:

'Sleep on, dear son, in a foreign grave - Mother'.

On that of a young lieutenant whose tablet is next to Sydney:

'Valiant heart, we thank God for every remembrance of thee'.

There is no personal message on Sydney's tablet. His record lives on in the scraps of paper from which this book has been written.

Sydney never lived to see the great Suvla Bay offensive launched on August 6th 1915 to revitalise the Gallipoli campaign. Fresh landings were made further up the peninsula, alongside the precarious hold of the Anzacs. After heroic sacrifices, these encountered stiff opposition and ground to a halt in the rugged terrain north of Sari Bair.

In December the War Office reviewed the situation and ordered an evacuation. This was carried out on the 19th-20th of December 1915 without a single loss of life.

Above: Sydney Hall's gravestone

Left: The author at the grave in 2008

Three years later, on the collapse of the Ottoman Empire and her withdrawal from the war, the allied fleets sailed unopposed through the Straits and occupied Constantinople. By now the war was over, the Sultan and pashas deposed and a new period of reconstruction and reconciliation begun by Kemal Mustafa, whose career really began with the Gallipoli campaign.

Unlike other theatres of war, no antagonism lingered between the combatants. Allied and Turkish troops developed an outspoken regard for each other, a recognition of each other's sterling qualities and steadiness, pluck and code of honour. Kemal Mustafa - 'Atatürk' - superbly caught this mood in his words of 1934, now inscribed on the war memorial at Anzac Cove:

'Those heroes that shed their blood and lost their lives ... You are now lying in the soil of a friendly country. Therefore rest in peace. There is no difference between the Johnnies and the Mehmets to us where they lie side by side here in this country of ours ... You the mothers who sent their sons from far away countries wipe away your tears; your sons are now lying in our bosom and are in peace. After having lost their lives on this land they have become our sons as well'.

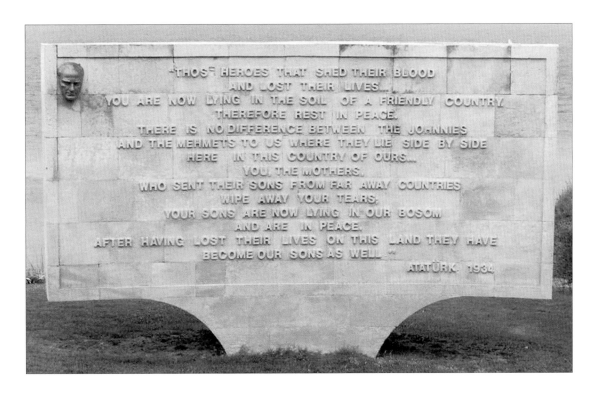

EPILOGUE

THEY SHALL GROW NOT OLD; the brief, brave sacrifice of a whole generation of young men lived on in the memories of parents, brothers, sisters, friends. Life went on. Members of the Hall family still live in Somerset.

Ben Hall never really recovered from the shock of Sydney's death. His health gave way completely and he died, a broken man, in 1919. By then Antony was 24 and competent to take over the farm. Clara Hall lived until 1938.

Two days after Sydney's death, Win had her baby - a boy - who was given his uncle's name. Sydney Evans, later followed by two sisters, became a very special favourite of Auntie Dor and when, in later years, he entered the ministry, she lived long enough to see him installed as Dean of Salisbury Cathedral.

Alfred Ball, Sydney's comrade-in-arms at Gallipoli, became a close family friend and frequently visited Fillwood. He came unscathed through the battles on the Western Front and married a sweet French girl whom he brought home to England where they raised a family. Moving house in about 1930, he climbed a tree to dislodge a radio aerial, sadly fell and broke his neck.

John Baghot de la Bere, after a spell of duty as a chaplain to H.M. Forces, left Bedminster. He never married.

Alfred Pearce got his commission and intended to make the Navy his career, but the Geddes axe (1923) put an end to that and he returned to civilian life. He became embittered and resentful, 'a changed man' said Dor, who must have given up any intention of marrying him long before that. Meanwhile, she had met Ralph Jefferis, a member of the New Zealand branch of the family, who was on active service on the Western Front. His leaves were spent at Fillwood, where he won all hearts, including that of Dorothy Hall.

He was the fifth son of Rowland and Mary Jefferis of Knowle Farm, Flag Swamp, Otago. Altogether there were seven sons and three daughters. Five of them died in the '20s, possibly of TB. The fourth son, Rowland Gordon, died of typhoid on a troopship on the way to the First World War.

After his second leave with them, Ralph sent Dor a silver locket engraved with his and her initials. 'I don't expect to come through this', he wrote from the Western Front. All the members of his company were wiped out. He was killed at the Battle of Passchendaele on 4th October 1917. 'If he had lived, I should have gone back to New Zealand with him', said Dorothy.

After that, though she was not short of looks, charm or opportunities, she put away any thought of marriage. She was too much attached to home, farm and family, and by a strange twist of fate, the children she should have had came to her as a result of another untimely death.

On 1st November 1919, Jean Page went upstairs to fetch a new dress she had made for her youngest daughter's birthday party, and fell dead from a brain haemorrhage. Captain Page, away at sea at the time, erected a monument over her grave in Westcliff cemetery. 'A better wife could not be found'. Mary Webb stepped into Jean's shoes and brought up the three Page girls, who utterly adored her.

The two youngest, Jackie and Hilda, came to Fillwood every summer with Mary, and Dor, with her energy and terrific sense of fun, threw herself into making these holidays totally memorable. The little girls were so captivated by the life of the farm - leading the horses, haymaking and other activities - that they spent the rest of the year at Westcliff 'playing Fillwood' until the summer came round again.

Everyone expected that Captain Page would marry Mary Webb, but that was not to be. For twenty years the widowed sea captain sailed the oceans of the world, returning now and again to see his little girls, and on one occasion he lost his ship by fire in the Indian Ocean. For twenty years Mary adored him from a distance.

On the outbreak of the Second World War, Captain Page considered removing his family to Canada - a move much dreaded by Mary. One day, while on leave, he said to her, 'Well, old girl, I've got a shock for you'. She braced herself for the news. 'I'm going to marry you'. She had more than deserved it.

Captain Page died in 1957 and Mary spent her last years in a nursing home. The three girls never married. Joan went to work with British Petroleum and first Jackie, then Hilda, became Anglican nuns, regularly visiting their beloved 'Auntie Dor', till she died at the age of 96 in 1987.

She was the last of Sydney's brothers and sisters. Antony married Dorothy Snook in 1926 and Dorothy Hall and her mother moved to Ostend Cottage, built for them on Gifford's Hill, Bishopsworth, by Uncle Edwin. He also helped Antony to buy Fillwood when the Temple Estate was sold up in 1924, but twenty years later the needs of expanding Bristol led to the compulsory purchase of Fillwood for building land, and Antony moved to Folly Farm, Tickenham.

Ostend Cottage is on the left

Fillwood Farm, first leased out by the Bristol Corporation, was vandalised, and by 1950 was quite derelict. The site was cleared and now nothing survives but part of the track from Novers Hill. Even the terrain has been altered by the building of Hengrove Way and the Knowle recreation ground. Most of Antony's descendants live in Clevedon, Somerset. Since the death of Dorothy Hall, they hold the papers and memorabilia relating to Sydney.

Edwin Wyatt, whose life and almanac is the thread that binds this story together, outlived them all. He continued to work at his office in town, to sing in the church choir, to be the very heart and soul of Bishopsworth until he died in harness at the great age of 97. That was in 1946, the year that another twenty names were added to the war memorial in St Peter's Church - but that's another story.

They shall grow not old,
As we that are left grow old.
Age shall not weary them
Nor the years condemn.
At the going down of the sun
And in the morning
We will remember them.

1914

1919

Bishopsworth Church.

THEIR·NAME·LIVETH·FOR·EVERMORE

This card is an expression of the appreciation of the PARISHIONERS of BISHOPSWORTH for the services rendered

by

in the Great War.

By sacrifice and suffering and death, he helped to protect our homes, keep our shores inviolate, and uphold the great truths of Freedom and Justice.

We commend him to the love of God, and offer our sincere sympathy to those who have been so grievously bereaved.

WAR DECLARED.   Aug. 4th 1914.
ARMISTICE GRANTED, Nov. 11th 1918.
PEACE SIGNED,   June 28th 1919.

INDEX OF PERSONAL NAMES

Adams, Clifford 51, 58, 63, 65, 69, 70, 73

Adams, George 58

Adams, Mabel (Mab) 32, 58, 74, 76

Baber 78

Baghot de la Bere, Rev. John 49-51, 53, 59, 62, 76, 78, 79, 83, 89, 96

Ball, Sgt Alfred J. 75, 92, 93, 96

Bannister, Rev. and Mrs 50

Bantock, Anton 1, 3, 5, 6

Beach, Sapper 93

Bellamy, Sam 80, 86

Birdwood, Gen. William 20, 42

Boulton 59

Britton, Amy 25, 68, 80

Britton, John 35, 69

Britton, Sarah 34, 35, 50, 59, 68, 80, 87, 89

Brock, Charles E. 6

Brooke, Rupert 68

Brown, Sgt 25

Budd 70

Bullock, Frank H. 91

Burges, Col. W.E. 7, 8

Butcher, Miss (m. Needham) 45, 60

Butterford, Dr 80

Caldwell, James (Mrs) 20

Carpenter, Stanley 32, 35-37, 43, 50, 58, 82, 89

Champain 50, 51

Chapman, Miss (m. Page) 47, 53, 67, 77, 80, 86, 89

Churchill, Winston 20, 78

Clarke, Gladys 78

Cockey 68

Cole 8

Cope-Proctor, Pvt 44, 49

Coutanche, André and Marie Jo 6

Cox, Clara 78, 82

d'Amade, Gen. Albert 20

de Robeck, Admiral Sir John 21, 24, 37

Dines, Cpl 79

Dunscombe (optician) 40

Egbester, Ernie 82

Evans, Jack 32, 37, 41, 59

Evans, Katie 69

Evans, Will 7, 29, 32, 37, 40, 41, 50, 52, 53, 54, 58-60, 64, 69, 73, 75, 76, 84

Findikoglou, Ali 5

Flower, Isabella 45

Ford, Mrs 7, 9, 51, 73

Ford, Revd 7-9, 30, 51, 52, 64, 69, 73, 75, 76, 77, 84, 86

Fox, Doctor 35

Franklin, Harold 50

Froud, Alfred 45

Froud, Hester Elizabeth (née Hall) 45, 59

Fry 48

Gardiner (family) 7, 30, 37, 52, 59, 74

Golding, Philip 9

Gough, Dennis 33, 54, 60, 62, 73, 75, 87

Gough, Mrs 73, 75, 76, 78, 87

Gouraud, Gen. Henri 65, 66

Grierson 33

Hale 49

Hall, Albert 9

Hall, Antony ('Son') 13-15, 17, 30, 32, 33, 40, 44, 45, 49-51, 53, 56, 58, 62, 63, 64, 69, 70, 73, 75-77, 79, 80, 82, 86, 89, 96-98

Hall, Benjamin (Ben) 11-13, 15, 17, 25, 27, 29, 31, 32, 35, 40, 45-47, 49, 53, 56, 58-60, 63, 70, 73, 74, 76, 77, 80, 84, 86, 87, 90, 91, 96

Hall, Clara (née Wyatt) 11-15, 19, 20, 25, 27, 29, 31, 34-36, 40, 41, 44-46, 49, 50, 53, 59, 62, 64, 67, 69, 70, 73-80, 82, 84, 86-92, 96

Hall, Dorothy ('Dor') 5, 8, 13-17, 22, 25, 26, 30, 32, 34-37, 40, 41, 44-46, 49-54, 56-60, 62-64, 67, 69-71, 73-77, 82-84, 87, 89, 90, 96-98

Hall, Maggie 50, 52, 62

Hall, Rhodney 32

Hall, Sydney (Syd) 5, 11-38, 40-50, 52-54, 56, 57, 58-60, 62-65, 67-71, 74-76, 78-80, 82-84, 87-94, 96-98

Hall, Winifred (Win, m. Evans) 7, 13, 15, 17, 23, 29, 32, 36, 37, 40, 41, 43, 50, 53, 54, 56, 58-60, 62-64, 67, 69, 73, 75, 76, 83, 84, 86, 89, 96

Hamilton, Gen. Sir Ian 20, 21, 24, 28, 29, 36, 39, 41, 44, 47, 48, 58, 65-67

Hensler 7

Hill, Cecil 9

Hill, Gerald 9, 89

Hill, Joe 9

Hill, P.C. 9

Hitchen, Horton 27, 58, 67, 70

Holbrook, Mrs 49

Hooper, Percy 82

Horler, Maud 82

Howe, Mrs 78

Hunter-Weston, Gen. Sir Aylmer 20

Irby, Esmé (Smyth) 26, 27

James, Sgt 44, 49

Jefferis (family) 31, 96

Jones 48

Keel, Cpl W. 89

Kidd, George 70

Langford 79, 87

Langridge 49

Lever, Stanley 63

Light, Joe 30

Lillington, Christine 6

Liman von Sanders, Gen. Otto 21, 39

Llewellyn, Col. 11

Lloyd George, David 84

Longridge 76

Lucas, Hilda 41

Lukins, Jack 9

Mallard, Miss 51, 87

Manson 25, 29

Marshall, Lieut 48, 79

Masefield, John 34, 38

Mathias, Anne 80

Mawson, Lieut 60, 92

May, Sapper 42, 62

McBain, Lieut 44, 45, 49, 62

McClelland 48

Millier, Blanche 30

Milward, Annie 69, 70

Moon (family) 7-9, 30, 32, 37, 40, 52, 60, 80

Moore, Len 82

Morgan (family) 63, 74, 75, 78, 87

Morgan, Maj. G.E. 88, 90

Munro, John 91

Murphy 74, 80

Mustafa, Kemal ('Atatürk') 95

Needham, Will/Willie 45, 60

Oakden, Lieut 54

Orr 15

Owen 50

Page, Capt. Will 25, 30, 31, 33, 36, 42, 43, 52, 63, 64, 97

Page, Hilda 97

Page, Jackie 97

Page, Jean (née McCulloch) 30, 31, 33, 40, 52, 60, 63, 64, 71, 82, 97

Page, Joan 97

Page, Rev. Theodore 47, 53, 77, 86

Paris, Gen. Archibald 20

Parsons, P.C. 73

Pavey, Amy 30, 53, 60, 69

Pearce, Alfred 32, 35, 37, 40, 46, 49, 50, 52, 53, 57, 62, 64, 67, 69, 70, 73-76, 87, 96

Pearce, Eddie 53

Pearce, Harold 35, 52, 62

Pitman, Alfred 46, 53, 74

Porch, Jim 70

Powell, Marion 64

Proctor, Thomas 44

Purdue 57

Quick, Reg 8, 9

Ran, Jai 15, 16

Randall, Mrs 12

Reynolds, Jack 80
Richards, Una Brookhouse 59
Ringham (family) 82, 83
Roberts 60
Robertson, Sgt 64
Robson 62
Roe, Lieut A.H. 60, 62, 79
Rogers 52
Rossiter 7
Ruddock, Sapper W.B. 22, 23, 52
Russell (family) 45, 59, 73, 87, 89
Sansom, John and Angela 6
Sharman 48
Simmons, Joe 9
Skinner 67
Smyth, Dame Emily 26
Snook, 'Floss' 69, 73, 77
Snook, Dorothy (m. Hall) 97
Snook, George 37, 63, 73, 75, 77, 86, 89
Spicer 48
Stanier, J. 48
Stevens, Belle (née Flowers) 40, 57
Sweet, Ernest 9, 59
Sweet, John 9
Taylor (family) 40, 76
Temple (family) 11, 35, 97
Thomas 58
Thomas, Dr 77
Tollust, Lieut 54
Verbyst, Joe 80
Vowles, J. 60
Warne, Ronald 57, 82, 83, 89
Webb, Ann 31
Webb, Mary 30, 31, 40, 52, 64, 70, 71, 97
Weeks 48
Wells, Lt-Cdr A. Randall 89, 90
Williams 48
Williams, Cass 70, 71
Wills, Sir George Oatley 49
Wincole, Sgt 79
Withers, Bill 17
Withers, Edith (Edie, née Snook) 27, 35,
   46, 62, 70, 73

Withers, Ernest (Ernie) 63, 75, 80, 86, 89
Withers, Ida 17, 26, 63, 70, 73, 75, 77,
   79, 83, 87
Withers, Lily ('Fido', née Britton) 34, 63
Withers, Lucy 32, 35, 45, 46, 51, 59, 69,
   73, 74, 76, 77, 83
Withers, Nell 50, 73
Withers, Richard (Dick) 27, 32, 35, 45,
   46, 51, 62, 70, 73-75, 77, 80, 86
Withers, Ruth 34, 37, 63, 77
Witt, Misses 52
Wyatt, Arthur 7, 27, 30, 45, 49, 57
Wyatt, Ben 27
Wyatt, Edwin Light 7-9, 11, 20, 28, 57,
   89, 91, 97, 98
Wyatt, Elizabeth (Lizzie) 7, 30, 76
Wyatt, John 14, 49
Wyatt, Joseph 12, 20, 52
Wyatt, Margie 13-16, 90
Wyatt, Phyllis 13
Wyatt, Phyllis (cousin) 34
Wyatt, Sydney 11
Yeomans 19